MW00380098

Table of Contents

PREFACE. XI

CHAPTER ONE 1
Let's Get the Bad News on the Table:
Romance Is Never Enough

CHAPTER TWO 9
What Partnership Would You Ever
Enter into without an Agreement?
Oh, Yeah ... Marriage

CHAPTER THREE 23
Resentments About Money Destroy
More Marriages Than Anything Else

CHAPTER FOUR. 35
Getting Naked Financially and Emotionally:
What Does Your Spouse Really Deserve
to Know About You, and Vice Versa?

CHAPTER FIVE 43

Planning to Pay off a Spouse's Debt, Purchase a Joint Asset with Your Money, or Cover Costs for a Married Child? Read This First.

CHAPTER SIX 53

Should You Let Your Spouse Stop Working?

CHAPTER SEVEN 63

What Happens to an Inheritance if a Marriage Doesn't Last?

CHAPTER EIGHT 71

Minding Your Own Business: How Much Does a Spouse Get in a Split?

CHAPTER NINE 79

If You're Fighting about Money, You're Really Fighting About Who's the Boss

CHAPTER TEN 89

Okay ... Now You Can Go Get Married

BEFORE YOU SAY "I DO" 93

Discussion Checklist

BEFORE THEY SAY "I DO" 99

Checklist for Parents of Children Getting Married

ABOUT THE AUTHOR 101

PREFACE

I do not profess to be an expert on marriage, nor do I have the "secret" to a perfect union. But I do have more than thirty-five years of experience as a divorce attorney, talking to clients whose marriages were at various stages of disintegration. From those many conversations, I discovered most of the issues that had torn apart their relationships stemmed from a lack of communication and understanding.

They said "I do" without really knowing their spouses' needs, desires, and values—and without expressing their own. Time after time, they lamented that if they'd had these discussions before or even during their marriage, perhaps they would not have wound up in my office. Moreover, this lack of communication didn't just affect them; it had a significant financial and emotional impact on their families as well.

One foolproof way to ensure that these crucial exchanges occur before marriage is to enter into a prenuptial agreement. But even if you are not signing a prenup, it's essential that you find ways to have them.

So many clients seeking a divorce confided in me that they buried their heads in the sand instead of heeding the warning signs that there was something wrong. They all wished they had given their marriage the attention it needed before it was too broken to fix. In addition, parents whose children were seeking divorces—and risked losing the value of their family businesses or their own investment in their children's marriages—told me that if they had known what was at stake, they would have spoken up earlier, too.

You cannot imagine how many people have showed up for a consultation for a divorce saying they thought that this would never happen to them. The points these clients shared about what they wished they had known has helped me personally and professionally, and I've done my best to pass on this wisdom to others. For years, friends and family have said, "You should write a book." When my own twenty-something children and their friends started asking me to share with them what I have learned as they embarked on their adult relationships, I was finally inspired to put pen to paper, the book you now hold in your hands, *That Will Never Happen to Us*. This book compiles more than three decades of insight on how to get a marriage off to the best possible start, avoid and resolve conflict in healthy and intelligent ways, and protect yourself from the worst-case scenario—a reality for more than half of American marriages. I truly hope it helps you avoid ever needing a divorce attorney like me!

Throughout the book, I share real-life scenarios to drive home the impact of the decisions you make before and during marriage and demonstrate some of the ways these choices play out in court. Names and identifying details have been changed to protect individuals and maintain attorney-client privilege.

CHAPTER ONE

LET'S GET THE BAD NEWS ON THE TABLE: ROMANCE IS NEVER ENOUGH

Most people contemplating marriage feel themselves swept away by love, physical attraction, and a sense of relief that they'll "never be lonely again." They look at the landscape of broken marriages and tell themselves it couldn't possibly happen to them. It's an astounding mindset, considering the divorce rate is over 50 percent in the US. If you're sitting next to a friend, it's either her or you.

The sad reality is that instead of happily ever after, half of American marriages end *unhappily*.

As a family lawyer with more than thirty-five years of experience, I've met with people of all ages, ethnicities, and backgrounds, and heard their stories. I've talked to couples negotiating the details of their divorces and brides- and grooms-to-be determining whether they needed prenuptial agreements (spoiler alert: they did).

The innumerable cases I've seen and the conversations I've had about marriage—and why it ends—have led me to the following conclusion: if people thought about, talked about, and addressed more of their issues before they got married, there would probably be less divorce.

If it were all laid out on the table beforehand, the logistics of marriage could be managed far better—and many of those logistics are tied to expectations.

IT'S ALL ABOUT EXPECTATIONS

Here's a scenario I've faced more than a few times: I'm sitting across from an engaged couple—let's call them Ellen and Blake—negotiating their prenuptial agreement. I'm representing Blake, and another lawyer is representing Ellen. I pose a simple question: "Do you expect that the bride-to-be will quit her job and stay home once children are born?"

At the exact same time, Blake says, "No," while his future bride answers, "Yes."

How did this discordance arise? How did the couple land in my conference room, ready to tie the knot, without having discussed this basic but crucial consideration? *They haven't had any real in-depth discussions about expectations.*

They've talked about having kids, but they haven't gotten to the *what happens when* questions concerning this issue—and likely many others.

The conversation then takes an inevitable turn—toward money. "I don't make enough to support both of us," says Blake. "And I don't want to be solely responsible for supporting our family. She has to work."

"Well, I don't want to work if I have children," Ellen responds. "I want to be home with them. I don't want to have to hire a nanny."

The couple is at an impasse. Blake is adamant that the bride keep working, even if they have children, and insists that it be written into the prenuptial agreement. Ellen states, over and over again, that she wants to be an at-home mom. Now what?

There is a laundry list of things to consider when it comes to marriage, many of which don't get talked about until it's too late. Potential deal-breakers like kids, family, values, prejudices, politics, lifestyle expectations, holiday customs, and even pets are not addressed before couples find themselves at the altar. People are presumably in love when they get engaged, but they haven't really dealt with the tough stuff—they haven't taken that love for a test drive on rough terrain.

People are on their best behavior when they're dating. But what happens after a few years, when it's no longer roses and romance? The day-to-day of marriage inevitably becomes less honeymoon hot tub and more wet towels on the floor. It's impossible to predict the curveballs life will throw at you. What if you have a special-needs child, or one of your parents gets sick and requires full-time care? What if one of you commits adultery?

You need to know what you're getting into, and that means covering all of these topics and more.

Living and traveling together, spending holidays with your partner, and getting to know his or her family will provide insight into who and what you're really committing to with those vows.

Caring for a pet or babysitting a friend's child together will show you how your beloved takes care of someone else. Weathering the most difficult of experiences, like financial hardship, a family illness, or death, will show you what your partner—and your relationship—is really made of.

Dating and being engaged are all wine and long walks on the beach. Marriage is reality. The more you can do to practice and prepare yourself for that reality, the better.

MONEY CAN CAUSE MAJOR ISSUES

From decades of experience as a divorce attorney, I can tell you that few things get more real in a marriage than money. I've seen couples discover—often too late—that they have different ideas, values, and, of course, expectations concerning money. The issues that can arise when it comes to finances are virtually unlimited: would you pay for your spouse to go to school, be it a college or graduate education, or perhaps even a law or medical degree? And what happens if they earn that degree and decide to say goodbye? More importantly, what provisions have you put in place to address such an outcome?

You may disagree on what's worth splurging on in the first place. For instance, should you send your daughter to an expensive private school, or will public school suffice? Does your eleven-year-old son need $200 sneakers, or would something cheaper serve just fine until he stops growing?

You may argue about who should spend on what. Just ask my client Melissa, who came to see me to discuss divorcing her husband, Matt. She said she knew they should have talked more about money before they got married because Matt's general attitudes about it had led to a number of major arguments. However, his most recent response had been the last straw.

When Melissa sought Matt's approval to use part of their marital savings to have some important dental work done—necessitated by poor dental hygiene as a child—Matt refused. He believed Melissa's *parents* should pay since they were the ones who had failed to provide their daughter with proper dental care when she was young. Melissa was horrified by his reaction, and as far as she was concerned, this money conversation—and their relationship—was over.

Many people keep their spouses completely in the dark about their finances. I can't tell you the number of times I've met with someone who wants a prenuptial agreement, and after explaining that one of the requirements of a prenup is full financial disclosure, the person looks at me as if I have two heads.

"What?" he'll say, aghast. "I'm not going to tell her what I have!"

"You mean you haven't already discussed your assets and liabilities with her?"

He hasn't, and he doesn't plan to. Instead, he'll make all the investments, pay all the bills, and provide her with an allowance so she can go to Starbucks or buy a pair of shoes. The only way she'll ever know what they've got—*sans* prenup—is through divorce when he's obligated by law to show her.

Here's an even worse scenario: he doesn't want to disclose how much debt he has.

Let's say the couple gets married and goes on their honeymoon, and when it's time to do the bills at the end of the month, the new husband says, "Well, we need to pay my student loan, my auto loan, my payment on my $50,000 credit card debt, and the loan my parents gave me to buy the condo we're living in."

Whether he lied actively or by omission, resentments start to build (especially if his wife doesn't have any debt), getting their marriage off to a shaky start. And without a prenup, if they get divorced in the future, after she's paid off his debt, she doesn't necessarily get any credit for it.

This is almost exactly what happened to my client, Michael, who found out two months after his marriage to Kristen that she had tens of thousands of dollars of credit card debt—a fact she had never revealed to him while they were dating or during their engagement. Michael felt she had betrayed him by withholding this information, and Kristen felt abandoned because of Michael's refusal to help reduce her debt. They both agreed it was a terrible way to start a marriage and that they could have avoided the situation by disclosing their respective assets and liabilities ahead of time.

In all of these scenarios, when one party does find out about the other's financial circumstances, it's too late. However, all of this information and more would have been revealed and addressed as part of the prenuptial agreement negotiations. This is the time to have the hard conversations, to share information that could prevent a fight six years and two kids down the line, when you find yourself with $50,000 in joint credit card debt, or clueless about how much money you have—or how much you're entitled to.

Life changes, and there are a million factors that can affect your relationship. It's worth it to address them now and to understand what they mean for your marriage—to hope for the best, but plan for the worst.

We'll cover some of those crucial topics here. This is a book of hard-won advice about how to have those tough but necessary conversations with your prospective spouse, so you don't end up one day as my client!

If you're thinking about getting married, whether it's for the first, second, or even the third time, this book will show you the issues that often destroy relationships and tell you what you can do about them right now to make sure your marriage has the greatest chance of success.

If you're already married, this book can help you educate yourself about the myriad complications that may come up over the course of your commitment—student loans, leaving your job, building a business—the *what if* questions that are bound to arise as life happens.

If you're a parent with children of marrying age—or embarking on a second or third marriage yourself—this book can help protect assets you have earmarked for your children and prevent you from making unintentional gifts to a former spouse (yours or theirs).

If you're ready to lay the groundwork for a solid union, read on. We've got work to do, but it will be worth it in the end—which is hopefully just the beginning.

CHAPTER TWO

WHAT PARTNERSHIP WOULD YOU EVER ENTER INTO WITHOUT AN AGREEMENT? OH, YEAH ... MARRIAGE

I n the business world, most partnerships are carefully negotiated from the start. What are the parties' responsibilities to each
other? What are their respective roles? How will money be distributed? What happens if one partner no longer wants to stay with
the business? The ins and outs are hashed out before the doors open,
the website goes up, or the deal is signed.

Ironically, the only partnership in which virtually none of
the important issues come up for discussion and agreement prior
to the "start date" often has the greatest impact on all parties
involved—marriage!

Couples enter into a marital partnership with a handshake (or
a kiss) and a wink—nothing in writing and no discussion of what
happens if it doesn't work out. That doesn't make sense when you
think about it. You can always dissolve a business, sell your share of a
partnership, or otherwise move on. But marriage is much more com-
plicated. Marriage involves everything—where you live; how you

earn, spend, and save money; your sex life; children; investments—you name it.

And the vast majority of people have only grazed the surface of these key concerns in life, if they've touched on them at all prior to professing their love—and abiding commitment—in front of two hundred of their closest friends and family members.

Doesn't it make sense to have some sort of written contract in place prior to entering into such a multifaceted commitment? That contract is called a *prenuptial agreement*, or "prenup," and yet most couples would never dream of discussing the idea. They think prenups are only for people with great wealth, or those who don't trust their partners. "A prenup is not romantic," they say, or, "Bad things will never happen to us!" They may even worry that the act of drafting a prenup dooms their marriage—but entering into a prenup does not cause divorce any more than drafting a will causes death.

And what if bad things *do* happen? Wouldn't it be sensible to think through some of these issues in advance?

Marriage is a brilliant, complex partnership, and it makes sense to discuss—and memorialize—your feelings about some of the key issues before you go into it. Even if you don't have great wealth (yet), and even if you completely trust your potential spouse, and vice versa, **you still need a prenup.**

A PRENUP PROTECTS

When it's done right, a prenup protects both partners, not just the "moneyed" one. And if nothing else, having the kinds of discussions necessary for a prenup encourages people to address issues they might not otherwise have considered *before* marriage—to have conversations that could save them a lot of money and heartache later on.

Much of what people fight about in a relationship has to do with money: *this is my money, this is your money, buy me this,* and so on. A prenuptial agreement can prevent much of that conflict because it spells out the way money is handled within the relationship. There shouldn't be any hard feelings about financial matters because, with a prenup, you've agreed to the terms ahead of time.

For example, a prenup might stipulate that the moneyed spouse will provide the non-moneyed spouse with a certain amount of cash every year while they are married. The spouse receiving that money doesn't have to use it all, and if they end up getting divorced, whatever is left belongs to the recipient.

Now, suppose the same couple has a prenup that says the husband is going to pay for everything during the marriage. Years later, when his wife wants cash to go to a spa for the weekend or to purchase a new pair of shoes, he can't tell her she has to use her own money for those expenses; the prenup has made it clear that she's under no obligation to do so. Addressing the issue of how much and for how long spousal support will be paid in a prenup is another example of how this contract protects both parties.

CASE IN POINT

My client Felicia realized the necessity of such stipulations in a prenup. She was preparing to marry James, someone much older and wealthier than herself. James had asked her to sign a prenuptial agreement that included, among other provisions, a clause stating that Felicia would not be gainfully employed during the marriage because James wanted her to be available to travel with him. As such, he would "fully support her while they were married."

Felicia had observed James's spending habits while they were dating and confided to me that she viewed James as a bit of a "tightwad." She was rightly concerned that, although he was agreeing to support her, they would find themselves constantly battling over her spending.

To avoid this, Felicia smartly negotiated a provision in the prenuptial agreement that prohibited James from vetoing her spending. Even smarter, Felicia negotiated another provision that required James to pay enough spousal support to permit her to maintain her current spending level for the rest of her life should they get divorced.

What would have happened if Felicia did not insist on these terms in the prenup and instead simply quit her job, relying on James's promise to cover her needs? Most likely, their marriage would have been fraught with arguments over Felicia's spending and resulted in a divorce that left her with no income of her own and fighting for spousal support.

MAKE BETTER DECISIONS

Many of the decisions that are made over the course of a marriage—continuing to work, taking different jobs, spending premarital or inherited money—can be better made if you know what happens in the event that you get divorced.

I recently spoke with a woman, Cheryl, in her late thirties who is learning this the hard way. She and her husband both worked when they first got married and had similar salaries. They've since had two children, and a year and a half ago her husband lost his job. He has put little effort into finding a new one and is content to spend his days lounging around the house while the nanny takes care of the kids. She's continued to work and do very well, but he has no income—and they don't have a prenup.

Now that they are considering divorce, Cheryl is at risk not only of losing primary custody of her children because she goes to work while he's at home but also of paying him spousal support. (It's important to note that child support and custody can't be addressed in a prenup since the state's determination takes priority—making it even more crucial to tackle the factors that *can* be managed.)

This was quite the revelation for her; she had never considered the consequences of not having a prenup.

"Well," I said, "He's not working. He has no income. You do— *ergo* spousal support." I thought Cheryl's head was going to spin right off her shoulders. If they had a prenuptial agreement that stated that each of them waived the right to seek spousal support from the other, she would not be in this position.

ADDRESS ANYTHING AND EVERYTHING

Almost every major life issue can be addressed with a prenup—even death. This often comes into play with older couples entering their second or third marriages. The prenup can name a healthcare proxy, as well as designate who will make decisions about the funeral and burial. In addition, a prenup can specify the assets a spouse does or doesn't get if you die when you're married, and potentially override state laws that would entitle him or her to a particular percentage of your estate. You can also determine whether the prenup supersedes your last will and testament, or vice versa.

I'm also seeing more and more parents pushing for their engaged children to get prenups. They want to protect the wealth they're planning to pass down, and a prenup can do that as well.

The terms of a prenup can also change as a marriage progresses. Sunset clauses allow the terms of a prenup to be modified or terminated at some point in the future. Other terms can be based on how long you are married. In some cases, this means the longer a couple is married, the more one spouse has to pay the other in the event of divorce. I once worked with a client who had agreed to pay an extra $100,000 to his wife on every third anniversary. Six months before year three, he was on the phone with me questioning whether the marriage was worth it.

A prenup can stipulate how assets and property will be distributed if there is a divorce. Maybe you own some real estate that you acquired prior to your union—a reality for many people as the average marrying age continues to climb. Your spouse may think he'll move right in and you'll simply add his name to the title, while you assume it will stay yours. But knowing that he's hopefully going to live there forever, put up curtains, and pay part of the real estate taxes, you may decide to compromise—and you'd outline that compromise in the prenup.

Let's say you have $100,000 in equity in the condo right now. After you marry, your spouse is going to work and contribute to the mortgage payments. You might say the first $100,000 of equity that you already have in your condo goes to you in the event of a divorce, and anything else is split down the middle.

Or you might say that your spouse will gain an equity interest in the condo as the marriage progresses. For instance, if you divorce in years zero through three, your spouse doesn't get any equity, no matter how much he contributes; in years three through five, he gets 5 percent, and so on. If you want to protect your investment entirely, your prenup would state that your spouse waives any rights to your condo, regardless of any contribution he makes—financial or otherwise.

There are other key marital assets and aspects of marriage that can be addressed through a prenup, such as:

- **Bridal shower and wedding gifts:** A prenup can indicate who gets what in the case of divorce. Many couples decide to keep the gifts from their respective friends and family members.

- **Businesses**: How the value of your interest in a business will or will not be distributed can be delineated in a prenup.

- **Rights afforded by cohabitation:** In some states, rights accrue to a partner who has cohabitated with a partner prior to marriage. A prenup can waive any rights that may have arisen by virtue of cohabitation.

- **Debt:** Debt and what to do about it—another big issue in many relationships—can also be managed with a prenup. Your agreement could say that any debt incurred on an individual's credit card is that person's responsibility, or that neither party will charge on the other's card without express permission. Or you may say that if one spouse (or his or her parents) pays off the other's student loan or credit-card debt, that money must be paid back in the event of a divorce.

- **Income:** Is it separate property, or is it marital? This too can be stipulated in a prenup.

- **Inheritances and gifts from third parties:** Under most state laws, if you commingle an inheritance or gift from a third party, it's considered marital property. A prenup can guard against that. Say I inherit $100,000 and use it to buy a beach house with my husband. With a prenup spelling out exactly what happens to my $100,000, I can go ahead and buy it, title it, and do with it what I please because the terms of the prenup will protect my money if things go south.

- **Insurance:** A prenup can indicate whether one party is responsible for maintaining insurance for the other and dictate what happens in the event of divorce or death.

- **Interspousal gifts:** If your wife gives you the car of your dreams for Christmas, you may assume it's yours for life. But depending on the state you live in, that gift may be considered marital property in the event of a divorce. The prenup can specify whether interspousal gifts are treated as marital property or not.

- **Long-term healthcare:** A prenup can address who pays for it, and whether the expenses related to one spouse's prolonged illness or disability are the other's responsibility.

- **Everyday living expenses:** A prenup can designate who covers what.

- **Expenses for prior spouses or children:** If you're getting married for a second time and you have an obligation to pay expenses for a prior spouse or children, a prenup can prescribe how those expenses are paid.

- **Pets:** If you can't imagine life without Roxie, a prenup provides the opportunity to make sure she stays with you, no matter what.

- **Professional fees:** You can prearrange who pays professional fees in the event of divorce, and whether one party can recoup the expenses he or she will incur if the other party challenges the validity of the prenup.

- **Retirement assets:** If you prefer that your retirement benefits go to someone other than your spouse, a prenup can make that possible. Your potential spouse can waive the right to be the beneficiary.

- **Taxes:** Prenups can address how tax returns will be filed— jointly or separately—and who will pay taxes on what. For example, you may stipulate that the party generating taxes through his or her income will pay them, or that they will be paid jointly.

- **Titles:** A prenup can also indicate how title will be taken to assets during the marriage—will it be taken solely in the name of the person who uses his or her money to buy it, or will it be taken in joint names, even if one person pays? And if there is a divorce, how will those assets be distributed between the spouses?

WHEN TO BRING IT UP

With the understanding that a prenup has the potential to make a big difference in both the quality and duration of your marriage, you may be wondering about the best time to broach the subject. When might be a good time to bring up this all-important document, especially considering that prenups get a bad rap?

Bring it up when things get serious. If you're in love and you think this person is "the one," go for it. I tell my clients to have these discussions before they are "officially" engaged; this is a good time to tell your partner you want a prenup and to outline the reasons why you think it's necessary. Maybe your family has a business, and you want to protect it for future generations, or maybe you have a child from a previous relationship. Or maybe you've simply witnessed the effects of divorce and want to make sure you're both able to manage no matter what happens. These are all valid reasons that your beloved should understand.

The worst thing you can do is stage an elaborate proposal and throw two engagement parties and a wedding shower before showing someone a prenup for the first time. Trying to negotiate the terms of a prenup while you're planning your wedding takes a lot of the fun and excitement out of the process. Besides, if you talk about your prenup shortly before your wedding, after you've picked out a venue, paid your deposits, and bought the dress, those circumstances could be considered duress—unfair constraints that could make a prenup unenforceable.

You need sufficient time to retain and consult with a lawyer and to understand the rights you may be waiving under the prenup you are being asked to enter into. You need time to disclose your financial circumstances to the other party so he or she can make an educated decision; you can't ask your future spouse to agree to something without knowing what you earn or vice versa—that's creating a document in the dark. For these reasons and others, drafting a prenup sooner rather than later is always best.

A tip on broaching the topic of a premarital agreement: tell your fiancé you want to make sure *both of you* are protected if things dissolve. He may reply that that would never happen, but guess what? Fifty percent of people who claim they will never divorce their spouses are not telling the truth. Sure, maybe they think they are, but life and relationships change.

A good response to someone insisting a prenup is a moot point? "If we're never going to get a divorce, then we'll never need it." Case closed.

FOLLOW THE LAW

Now that we've discussed what can go into a prenup and when to raise the subject, there are a few things to keep in mind if you want to guarantee its validity. If you were negotiating the details of a new business, you wouldn't write your partnership agreement on the back of a napkin and say, "Uh, this looks good. Let's go with this." You wouldn't Google "business partnership agreements" and just pick one at random from the results and fill in the blanks.

Drafting a prenup is complex. Each state has its own laws pertaining to prenuptial agreements, so you need to find out what the law is in your particular state. **If you don't follow the state laws governing what is required for a prenup, it's not worth the paper it's written on.**

You have to know what the laws are in order to be sure that you're entering into a valid and enforceable agreement, and that means you need to consult with an attorney.

It's certainly worth the investment to pay a lawyer now, because if you get divorced without a prenuptial agreement—or if someone could easily question the validity of the one you have—you'll pay one much more down the line.

Having legal representation gives *both* parties more control. Otherwise, the person with the money has the most power to push things in the direction he or she wants. Each person having his or her own attorney levels the playing field.

MAKE SURE YOU AGREE

It's crucial to remember that both parties must agree to the terms of the prenup, and not just on paper. The prenup must represent a meeting of the minds, and it must be considered fair and equitable by both partners. Otherwise, it will cause problems rather than resolve them. Remember our couple from chapter 1, Ellen and Blake, who were negotiating their prenup and debating whether Ellen should stay home if they had kids? Ellen went along with Blake's stipulation that she would keep working, no matter what. Why? She might have thought that she could change his mind down the road, or that he'd waver from his stance if they had kids. Or maybe she figured that if she wanted to get married, she'd have to do what he wanted—and she was in love, so it was worth the sacrifice.

Either way, she signed on, despite the fact that she didn't *really* accept the terms. They got married, and soon their first child was born. As Ellen neared the end of her maternity leave, she was sure she didn't want to go back to work. She told Blake she didn't mean what she'd said in the prenup. He told her he did.

Now she has two choices: to continue working or to get divorced after having a baby. Even if she goes along with the prenup's provisions, her discontent will build. They'll fight about her working, and about other things, too—all because she entered into an agreement she wasn't comfortable with.

People often enter into agreements they don't actually *agree with* because they want to get married at any cost. But if you accede to your partner's terms just to get married, your frustration with those terms is unlikely to subside after your vows. It will build into one of the most significant barriers to marital bliss: resentment.

And don't just sign assuming you'll be able to change your partner's mind afterward. Trust me, rarely does anyone change his or her mind afterward.

This is also a good time for compromise: there should be give and take throughout the process. If you don't agree with your partner's position, work with him or her to find common ground. If you can't compromise now, imagine what your married life will be like.

If your parents—or your future spouse's parents—are pushing for a prenup, now is a good time to think about what they're asking for—and about the role they'll play in your relationship in the future. Many millennials are the products of helicopter parenting, and if you or your spouse are among them, your parents' meddling is going to have an impact on your relationship. If you're old enough to get married and have children, you're old enough to negotiate your own prenup and draw your own boundaries. You're the one who has to live with your spouse and the contract you agree to, and that means *you as a couple* must maintain control.

The best thing you can do with a prenup—after ensuring that you both truly agree to the terms and that it's legal, of course—is put it in a safe deposit box and never think about it again. But the discussions you've had while negotiating it, and the terms you've arrived at together, should serve as a decision-making guide throughout your marriage—saving you conflict and confusion along the way.

Next, we'll get into one of the biggest issues married couples face—money—and discuss ways to avoid money issues and the corresponding rifts they can cause in your relationship.

CHAPTER THREE

RESENTMENTS ABOUT MONEY DESTROY MORE MARRIAGES THAN ANYTHING ELSE

W hat triggers divorce? Is it couples growing apart? Stress related to raising children? Infidelity? The surprising reality is that I see more couples torn apart by money than all other issues combined. Who earns it, who spends it, and what it gets spent on are often the most dangerous topics when it comes to keeping a relationship alive and healthy. And like many marriage killers, it starts even before the first chime of those wedding bells.

When couples are dating and completely head-over-heels in love, everything seems perfect. It all just clicks. They have the same interests, the same desires—it seems as if the stars have aligned to bring them together. Consequently, they assume their values will also be completely compatible where money is concerned. This is rarely the case.

We all enter relationships with different backgrounds, experiences, and social conditioning when it comes to money, and that universe of circumstances shapes our financial thought system. As such, it's unlikely you and your spouse-to-be are as aligned as you think.

Often, couples haven't dug deep enough to discover the discrepancies in their beliefs before they marry. Or they stay mum about serious money issues—for instance, one partner may fail to reveal pertinent information about his financial life, fearing his fiancée would break off the engagement if she knew the truth about his excessive spending habits or four-figure credit card debt.

Even when money issues are out in the open, people fool themselves into thinking they'll be able to change their partners' ways. They imagine that once they're safely bound by matrimony, the difficulties or differences will dissipate. Believe me when I tell you they won't.

Moreover, the discrepancies in your financial perspectives and habits matter a great deal: so much of what goes on in a marriage—in a life—is about money. *What are our financial priorities? What kind of lifestyle are we going to have? Where can we save?* Without extensive discussion and disclosure about what you have, what you don't, and what you want your future to look like *before* you say "I do," resentments about money are bound to ensue.

Acrimony over finances frequently arises from:

Conflict Over Control

Resentments often build as a reaction to one spouse's attempts to control the other's spending. I've seen many cases in which a working spouse provides his non-working wife with an allowance or gives her a credit card with a low limit. No one likes to be treated like a child—and it's often only a matter of time before she lashes out.

On the other hand, she may be so concerned with "keeping up with the Joneses" that she is unrealistic about the family's budget. She'll push him to spend more and tell him he's inadequate when he can't make enough money to compete with the neighbors. In addition to feeling unappreciated, it sparks the "not good enough" syndrome, in which he feels he can't do anything right. In time, divorce begins to seem like the only viable option.

Concern About Equal Contributions

Perhaps you are a teacher, earning $50,000 per year, while your wife brings in $250,000 as an anesthesiologist. When one spouse makes significantly more money than the other, resentments can easily crop up.

If you care for your kids full time while your partner works outside the home, the same tensions can arise. You may be putting in just as many hours as your spouse, but you'll never be able to contribute at the same level financially—and if he or she believes you shouldn't be spending equally, it's easy to get frustrated.

Further, if your arrangement differs from what you've pictured— say you imagined you'd always be a two-income household, and your wife quits her job shortly after having your first child—it's easy to feel bitter. You might imagine she spends all day getting her nails done, going out to lunch, and playing tennis while you're hard at work. On the flipside, she feels resentful because you don't appreciate all she does to take care of the kids, keep the house clean, and make sure dinner's ready when you arrive.

Sometimes grudges over your arrangement can sneak up on you, even if you agreed on them at the outset of your marriage. People pat themselves on the back for making so much money that their spouses don't have to work, but eventually they come to resent it. I've seen many a high-wage earner who was initially proud that he could support the household on his own *and* hire a nanny, housekeeper, and cook to take care of his wife's every need. But by the time he arrives at my office, he's angry that she's not contributing and ready to let her fend for herself.

Providing as Much as His or Her Spouse's Parents Did

When one spouse is from a wealthy family, she may be disappointed that she and her husband can't afford the endless stream of new stuff that mommy and daddy used to buy her. Here, too, the "not good enough" syndrome can rear its ugly head.

He gets up at five o' clock in the morning to commute into the city, works all day under ridiculous pressure from his boss or business partner, and comes home at seven only to hear a barrage of complaints about how they don't have enough. When every day becomes a losing battle, eventually he's going to want out.

Spending Priorities

People have different ideas about how money should be allocated. Are you interested in buying a nice house, or more concerned with ensuring a long, stress-free retirement? Is there something else you think should take precedence, like saving for your children's education? What if your spouse doesn't feel the same way? Spending priorities pull couples apart all the time.

One of the financial topics couples fight about most is how much they should spend on their children. Should you gift your freshly licensed seventeen-year-old a new BMW, or will a hand-me-down Honda from your in-laws do just fine? Do you believe a private school education is invaluable, or is the local public school just as good? Should you send your kids to work at a summer job, or on a sightseeing trip for teens? Perhaps most importantly, are you footing the bill for college, or do you believe your children should learn responsibility by paying their own way? If you and your spouse don't share values in this arena, the disparity can be hard to reconcile, and it can cause a major rift in your relationship.

Secrecy About Money

I can't tell you how many times someone has come into my office without a clue about how much money she and her husband have. She doesn't know what's in the bank: all their accounts are in his name, and the statements go to his office. She's also unsure how much he earns; at tax time, he covers up the numbers on their return before she signs. She'll let this go on just to keep the peace ... until things start to go bad. When she realizes she needs access to those numbers, and her husband refuses, the feeling of being a trapped 1950s housewife is enough to send anyone over the edge.

The impact of these resentments is significant. When the playing field doesn't feel level in a marriage, people attempt to reclaim their power in other ways. If she feels she doesn't have control in her relationship because he won't share his financial information, she may have an affair as a way of asserting control over herself. Or he may feel underappreciated because nothing is ever good enough, and he may act out by sleeping with someone else. One partner may decide to withhold sex entirely—lack of sex in a relationship often occurs not because one partner is disinterested or undersexed, but because he or she is attempting to reassert himself or herself.

The couple may find themselves going tit for tat—he argues that if she drives a Mercedes, he should, too, or she decides that if he plays golf every week, she needs to visit the spa with the same frequency.

None of these outcomes is appealing, and all of them can lead to divorce. So, what can you do about it?

COMMUNICATION IS KEY

Many people wait until it's too late—until the resentments have already arisen, until they build and build and eventually blow. But the buildup occurs due to lack of communication.

Talking about these issues and expectations goes a long way; when the issues that cause tension are regularly discussed—before and *during* the marriage—you don't give them the opportunity to get out of hand.

Our lifestyles are deeply connected to money and how we choose to spend it, and it's essential to spell out what's important. When you go on vacation, would you rather allocate your budget to a first-class flight or to meals at fantastic restaurants? When purchasing a home, would you rather buy a $750,000 house with a $600,000 mortgage, or a $450,000 place and owe just $300,000? Spelling out what matters to you in terms of spending will make a difference in the choices and compromises you make as a couple, and help you avoid conflict.

For instance, I have a colleague whose husband was in a high-paying job that he hated, while she had a job that she thoroughly enjoyed. He began acting angry and resentful toward her, which she smartly recognized as being job related and not about her at all. As such, she insisted that they talk it through, and knowing how miserable it made him, she encouraged him to leave that job and pursue something he was passionate about. He took her advice and opened up his own firm. He's not making the same kind of money, but he's so much happier that they both agree the switch was worth it.

In addition to regular conversation, here are some steps you can take to prevent common grievances from reaching a point of no return:

- **Put together a prenup:** When you've stipulated *what happens when* in the relationship—who is working and will continue to work, how money and information will be shared, and more, the majority of important concerns have already been hashed out (provided that you were honest about your feelings and priorities during the process of drafting it, of course). While the prenup won't eliminate conflict, it gets everything out in the open to begin with and can serve as a guiding set of principles when disagreements arise.

- **Engage in estate planning:** Many people are hesitant to do this because they don't want to think about the inevitable. But death is, indeed, inevitable, and—as we touched on in the previous chapter—drafting a will, obtaining life insurance (which is smart to do when you're young and life-insurance premiums are accordingly low), and creating other end-of-life plans won't *make* you die. What it will make you do is have the important conversations inherent in the process.

- **Find a financial advisor:** Going to a financial advisor—a professional who provides strategies and services to help you navigate your financial life and achieve any money-related goals, such as purchasing a house or saving for your children's college tuition—before and during your marriage will also help with some of these issues. In order for the advisor to do his or her job, both of you must attend the meetings, and everything must be laid out on the table. This encourages uncomfortable conversations in a neutral environment while unearthing any outstanding debt, unhealthy purchasing habits, and the like. Your advisor can then provide cut-and-dried information and advice on how you should be spending and saving, thereby ensuring everyone is on the same page. And if you are engaged and determine you can't live with your spouse-to-be's money values because they're too different from your own, it's best to find out now.

- **Make room for a relationship counselor:** Like a financial advisor, a relationship counselor can serve as an impartial observer, helping you see your partner's perspective and find common ground.

CASE IN POINT

To see how these issues and solutions (or lack thereof) can play out, consider the real-life case of Tom and Andrea.

My client, Tom, grew up in a working-class family and spent ten hours a day at a stressful job. His wife, Andrea, was raised by wealthy parents and took care of their three children as a stay-at-home mom.

Andrea often complained about Tom's long work hours and accused him of being a "bad dad" because of his lack of involvement with the children. Simultaneously, she was frustrated that Tom didn't make enough money to provide them with a more extravagant lifestyle. She repeatedly brought up to Tom that her parents had given her a better life growing up than she had now.

Meanwhile, Tom was always worried about money and about how they'd put three children through college. To manage his anxiety and take control of their finances, Tom put Andrea on an "allowance," providing her with a set amount each week to cover her and the children's expenses. Andrea was unhappy with this arrangement and secretly received additional funds from her parents so she could spend as she wished. Meanwhile, Tom began having an affair with another woman to make him "feel better about [him]self."

The couple fought constantly about who was the better parent and whose money values were more appropriate. Eventually, Tom discovered that Andrea's parents were supplementing her spending, and Andrea found out about Tom's affair. Soon afterward, they sought a divorce.

As the case proceeded, it became evident that a great deal of resentment had built up over the course of the marriage. Tom and Andrea had not discussed their values about money or savings either before or during the marriage, and now it was too late.

From Tom's perspective, their breakup was Andrea's fault because:

- Andrea complained that they didn't have enough money, but never offered to get a job to help supplement their income.

- Andrea did not appreciate that the reason Tom could not spend more time with their children was that he worked so hard to satisfy her financial demands.

- Andrea "emasculated" Tom by asking her parents for money, and—worse yet—did so behind his back.

- Andrea was "spoiled" by her parents and was not a "good mom" because she was "overindulging" their children in the same way.

From Andrea's perspective, Tom was at fault because:

- Tom treated her "like a child" by putting her on an allowance.

- Tom did not respect her opinions or values about money, or her hard work in the home, because she did not bring in a paycheck.

- Tom was not justified in being angry with her for receiving money from her parents because he was not providing enough for her to live the lifestyle she desired.

- Tom was a "bad dad" because he put work before his children, and a "bad husband" because he cheated on her.

The following considerations and actions from both parties potentially could have saved their marriage:

- Recognizing that they grew up in different worlds, the couple should have discussed their expectations regarding working, spending, and saving prior to getting married. If they had a prenuptial agreement, all of these issues would have been addressed and documented up front.

- Before Andrea asked her parents for money and before Tom started his affair, an honest and open discussion (perhaps with the assistance of a marriage counselor) might have cleared up many of their festering resentments and put them on a different path.

- Having a third-party "referee" is especially helpful when a couple has such divergent views about money. Tom and Andrea could have hired a financial advisor to counsel them on possible compromises and help them set common goals. Sometimes a financial counselor can be even more important than a marriage counselor.

- Tom and Andrea could have acknowledged that neither of them really thought the other was a "bad" parent; rather, they used the insult as a way to hurt each other's feelings, even though the root cause of their frustration was financial.

Money matters dictate so much of our lives. Recognizing your financial differences, knowing what you're getting yourself into, agreeing about the terms of your life together, and airing any grievances as they come up are essential as you navigate the choppy waters of marriage. And maintaining honesty, compromise, and consideration for the person you professed your undying love to will surely aid your cause along the way.

Now that you understand the impact of financial differences and ways to manage them, we'll discuss what you should know about your fiancé before making one of the biggest commitments of your life.

CHAPTER FOUR

GETTING NAKED FINANCIALLY AND EMOTIONALLY: WHAT DOES YOUR SPOUSE REALLY DESERVE TO KNOW ABOUT YOU, AND VICE VERSA?

What do we really need to know about someone before we commit? That he or she is a kind person who loves animals and moonlit walks on the beach? All of that is terrific, but what if the person you're planning on marrying has $20,000 worth of credit card debt or $100,000 worth of student loan debt, hasn't told you, and isn't planning to tell you until after the honeymoon? What if he hates kids, while you can't imagine your life without them? What if she struggles with addiction and doesn't plan to disclose it?

Some people are willing to get naked with each other as early as the first date, and others wait until the wedding night—but both types of people can find it extremely hard to "get naked" with each other in other ways. However, it's essential that you do, and that you do it before the big day. I've seen what happens when everything isn't revealed up front; I've heard "I should've known" more times than I can count.

I should've known he wouldn't take responsibility for our kids because when we had a puppy, he'd never take it out.

I should've known she had a short fuse when she screamed at me for not booking first class for our honeymoon flights.

I should've known he had a problem with alcohol when I saw all those empty bottles in his bedroom while we were dating.

You should never have to say, "I should've known," because you have the opportunity to know it now.

By engaging in experiences that are more challenging than long walks on the beach, ones that emulate the everyday difficulties of living alongside someone else—for better or for worse—you'll get more insight into who you're marrying, how they handle conflict, and what your partnership might look like down the line.

Here are some suggestions for how to test the bounds of your seemingly endless love before you get married:

Experience Adversity

During that magical time of courtship, when everybody's getting along, the car is humming along without a hitch, and your money issues are your own, the relationship naturally feels perfect. But when adversity arises, perhaps in the form of an illness, a shortage of cash, or a problem with your sex life, how does your fiancé deal with it?

Does he shut down, or become defensive or aggressive? These are important tells about how he'll handle the big issues that will inevitably arise in your marriage, so it's important to test the waters.

Go on Vacation

If you travel to a beautiful tropical island with your one true love and everything goes according to plan, your relationship remains flawlessly intact. But what if your flight gets cancelled, and you have to sit in the airport for twenty hours? What if one of you gets food poisoning, or so sunburned you can't be touched, or needs to go to a hospital? How does your fiancé weather the disappointment that her perfect vacation is ruined? The inevitable difficult moments during your trip—whether few or frequent—will provide a preview of what your relationship may look like when real life hits.

Get to Know Your Future In-Laws

Before you get married, your future in-laws may be on their best behavior, treating you like one of their own. As such, it can be hard to see what you're getting yourself into. Alternatively, if they aren't so nice, don't think *"maybe they'll be better after we get married or after we have children."* If anything, things will probably get worse.

When it's the man or woman of your dreams we're talking about, you may wonder why it matters what their parents are like. **But you're not just marrying your spouse; you're marrying his or her family, too.** Any quirks or points of contention will be amplified once you're officially in the mix and spending weekly dinners and holidays with these strangers-turned-kin. If in-laws are hovering over your future husband, you may be subject to their opinions about you—how you spend your money, how you raise your children, when and where you vacation, and so on—for the long haul. Can you deal with that? Your mother-in-law certainly won't stop meddling just because you're married. A heart-to-heart discussion with your future mother-in-law now will be a good indicator of whether she will be an outlaw once you're married.

Talk About the Possibility of Pets and/or Children

Are you the kind of person who picked out your future kids' names in first grade, or would you rather that children be kept out of sight until they turn eighteen? Does the name of your first pet serve as all of your Internet passwords, or does the bark of a dog four blocks away make you nervous? How does your fiancé feel about children and pets?

Like most personal preferences, these considerations stir up strong feelings, and they are not likely to change. The same goes for the morals and values you plan to impart to your offspring, should you choose to have them—like those we mentioned regarding spending.

You can test how your significant other will really be when a child or pet comes along by babysitting for someone else's child or fostering a pet. If you do not like the way he or she cares for, disciplines, or shows affection during the trial run, there's still time to discuss and work on these problems. Ignoring them won't make them go away.

Compare Your Values When it Comes to Money

If you had unlimited funds, would you rather live in a huge penthouse or a little cottage off the grid? Money and how we spend it affects virtually every aspect of our lives, and if you're not on the same page, you need to figure out how to get there or decide whether it might be better to part ways.

Consider opening a joint bank account, with each of you contributing a share based on your individual incomes and see if you're able to agree on how that money will be spent on expenses that will benefit you equally—like a vacation!

Determine Whether Your Political and/or Religious Views Align

Strong feelings and beliefs can cause rifts in a relationship when they're not mutual. Determining whether you agree about the ideals that are most dear to you—and whether any misalignment may cause significant issues for your connection—is always a good idea.

Check Out Their Work Ethic

Work ethic can be an indicator not only of your future spouse's drive for professional success but also of how he or she will tackle the struggles that occur in a marriage. Will your spouse carry his share of the household chores, bill-paying, and other not-so-fun activities that need attending to during the marriage, or will he seek to put those burdens on you? Will he quit his job without worrying about the pressure that puts on you (remember Cheryl from chapter 2)? Asking whether he worked or was required by his parents to do chores and contribute to other family responsibilities growing up—and observing how he handles certain "jobs" (personal and professional) while you're dating or engaged can be a good indicator of how he'll perform after "I do."

Ask About His or Her Physical and Mental Health History

Our health affects everything we do, and your partner's current mental and physical health, as well as his or her family's health history, will have an impact on your life together.

If you're planning to have kids, this issue is even more pressing, as you'll be passing on his or her genes along with your own. Knowing about any risk factors enables you to be fully informed about some of the most important decisions you'll make, like the well-being of your future children.

Notice Sexual Compatibility or Dysfunction

Nowadays, the majority of couples have sex before they're married. If it isn't good, don't ignore it; it won't just get better once your bed becomes marital.

And look out for the way your partner deals with any dysfunction or dissonance sexually. It's an indicator of how they'll address this vital issue and other touchy subjects till death (or divorce) do you part.

Paying attention to the considerations listed above will help you determine whether you're truly compatible. But beyond discovering a shared affinity for cats or the joint desire to retire early, you should also look for characteristics in your beloved that don't bode well for managing the tough stuff in life. The following qualities are worth looking out for (and are also not likely to change):

- **Jealousy:** If you're at a party, making the rounds while your fiancée sits by herself, is she likely to be upset or accuse you of flirting with someone else at the end of the night? If you're both lawyers and your spouse is more successful, are you going to feel jealous and resentful? Think about how this may play out over time.

- **Road Rage:** If your spouse-to-be has a penchant for slamming on the gas pedal and shouting obscenities at other drivers, is it possible he has an anger-management issue? This behavior is going to translate to other areas of your life together, and it won't just be third parties on the receiving end of his anger. If he flies off the handle when a car cuts him off, what's he going to do when you burn dinner?

- **Lack of Self-Control:** Are there signs that your partner has an addictive personality? Have you noticed a tendency to overindulge in food, drink, or even pornography? For many of the people I see with spouses facing addiction issues, the problems started long before they met. While the issue was visible while they were dating and engaged, he or she thought somehow it would stop. Generally, that doesn't happen—at least not without recognition that the problem exists and willingness to get help for it.

- **Secrecy, Again:** If someone is not willing to talk to you about money—or anything else, for that matter—that's a big red flag.

It's easy to mask issues for a little while or to assume you can address and change them in the long run. But these problems are often hard—if not impossible—to effectively solve.

Test the waters as much as you can. Go to a party, foster a pet, babysit a friend's child, ask your partner if they've ever had a serious relationship with alcohol or dangerous substances, and pay attention to what you hear and observe.

After collecting this important data, it's crucial to absorb and believe it. Realize that none of what you see is likely to shift, especially not without third-party intervention. Whatever you do, don't bury your head in the sand. Addressing anything negative up front gives you the best chance of overcoming it ... or at least avoiding some of the heartbreak and expense if it can't be resolved.

Of course, you have to prioritize, too—no one's perfect, and neither is anyone's relationship. I'm not telling you to break up with your partner if you unearth something that isn't optimal; only you can decide on your must-haves and deal breakers. However, you need to know what you're working with so you can make a plan to address it or decide it's time to move on.

Once you've bared all and determined that you're on board with everything you've uncovered, we'll talk a bit more about finances— namely, your or your parents' contribution toward big expenses, like an advanced degree for your spouse, a home, or paying off debt.

CHAPTER FIVE

PLANNING TO PAY OFF A SPOUSE'S DEBT, PURCHASE A JOINT ASSET WITH YOUR MONEY, OR COVER COSTS FOR A MARRIED CHILD? READ THIS FIRST.

One of you has some savings and the other is embarking on graduate or professional school. Doesn't it make sense for the spouse with savings to pay for the other spouse's education? Well ... maybe. What if the relationship doesn't last? In that case, one spouse has the degree and the earning power, and the other's savings have been depleted. Is that fair?

What about paying off your soon-to-be son- or daughter-in-law's student loans so the couple can enter into marriage debt-free? How about helping your child and his spouse buy a home or a car? Perhaps you're more than happy to help them get their life together off to a good start, but what if that relationship ends? In that case, would you feel as good about your generosity? While it is fine to give such a generous gift if the couple remains married, do you really want your ex-daughter-in-law to benefit from your kindness (perhaps to your own child's detriment) if she divorces your son just a few years down the road?

Anytime you make a financial decision with a spouse, married child, or son- or daughter-in-law, you have to think about the possibility of divorce. It sounds very unromantic and impersonal, but think about it this way: if you think the world of your spouse today, but next week you find her in bed with her lab partner, are you going to feel the same way about having paid for her tuition? Or, as a parent, would you feel as good about your gift knowing your daughter's ex could walk away with half the value of the home *you* bought after he divorces her?

It's a fine line between love and hate, and those scenarios could certainly drive you toward the latter.

Again, you can say, "That won't happen to us!" But it *does* happen—all too frequently, as my case files will attest! So, let's talk about what agreements may be necessary prior to embarking on that sort of financial path. Whether you're providing for your fiancé's tuition, paying off your daughter-in-law's debt, or helping your child purchase a home for her family, make sure you take the following steps to protect your investment.

IF YOU'RE THE SPOUSE OR SPOUSE-TO-BE

Say you're planning to support your future husband through school once you get married. You'll cover his tuition with your premarital savings, too, thinking that once he graduates, his newfound earning power will be well worth the investment.

Before making such a commitment, consider all the costs that come with schooling: books, study guides, exams, and especially the loss of income that occurs when one spouse stops working to attend school. While his education may very well pay dividends later, you need to fully understand what you're spending—and sacrificing—up front. Most importantly, you have to guard your investment so that a divorce won't leave you with lost savings and an inability to share in the upside.

If you're going to support your spouse or future spouse's education with your premarital money or by making significant financial compromises during your marriage, you should have a pre-nuptial or marital agreement that protects you in the case of divorce. Such protections could be in the form of a divorce-contingent reimbursement for the savings and/or income you used. Or it could be a requirement that your now-educated spouse pay a greater amount of spousal support over a longer period of time if you divorce to "repay" you for the time, money, and sacrifices you made to get him to where he is now.

YOU CAN'T COUNT ON THE COURTS

Why is it so important to have something in writing?

You can't count on the courts to rule in your favor, even if the case seems cut and dried. If you support your wife while she works on becoming a lawyer, and shortly after graduation she asks for a divorce, the situation might seem blatantly unfair, but there are arguments on both sides.

When faced with a divorce, it is amazing how two people in a relationship have two very different (and selective) recollections of what actually occurred in that relationship.

The now-educated spouse recalls that she worked summers at a law firm part-time and her parents helped pay for her law school tuition, while her husband did little to nothing to support her—financially or otherwise.

The supporting spouse remembers that it was *his* savings, *his* income, and *his* dedication to maintaining the household that allowed her to earn her degree. Either way, it is hard to prove who is "right"—it is quite challenging to formally account for who paid what, not to mention the intangible contributions that are impossible to tabulate. There are only two people behind the closed doors of the marital home; in the eyes of the courts, it's a veritable *he said, she said*, and their task is to pick the most plausible story.

CASE IN POINT

My client Jon experienced this firsthand when his wife of ten years, Rebecca, left him. He felt horribly used and betrayed, and he couldn't believe she was saying goodbye "after all [he] had done for her."

When the parties got married, Rebecca was just starting her first year of law school. Jon told me he worked while Rebecca was in school, providing their sole income while paying for her tuition with his savings. He supported her through the lean years and long hours of her first six years as an associate, taking care of their home and their young children all by himself.

Now that Rebecca had been made partner at her law firm and was making a substantial salary, she didn't want to be married to Jon any longer. Jon wanted spousal support from Rebecca as compensation for his time, effort, and financial investment—as well as additional money for her partnership interest, which he felt he helped her earn.

Rebecca's perspective on their respective contributions to the marriage was much different from Jon's. Rebecca felt that she had done "everything," while Jon simply faded into the background. In Rebecca's mind, *she* was the one who did it all on her own, working the hardest while taking care of the domestic responsibilities Jon claimed he had covered. And while Jon had paid for her to go to law school, she felt she'd made up for that with the significant income she had earned and contributed to the family during her past two years as a partner.

At no time before or during the marriage did Jon and Rebecca discuss their opinions on—or the implications of—Rebecca going to law school and Jon paying for it, or who would take care of the kids and the house. Life "just happened." Neither of them had any idea how the other was feeling, and as a result, their resentments grew unchecked. Each one felt the other was "taking advantage" and "not working as hard."

Could they have done things differently throughout their marriage, thereby preventing Jon from winding up in my office altogether?

Well, both parties would have benefited from a prenuptial agreement, because it would have addressed—at the very least—the payment of law school tuition, Rebecca's future partnership interest in her firm, and spousal support. As we discussed, using a prenup to help lay ground rules for a marriage and the life events that come with it ensures everyone knows where they stand, no matter the circumstances.

In addition, either party could have brought up their feelings of inequity when they first arose. By opening channels of communication, they could have prevented tensions from reaching a boiling point. Or the couple could have sought support from a marriage counselor to help them discuss any dissonance within their relationship, including the fact that they each felt they were carrying the bulk of the burden.

Instead, Jon and Rebecca are left to fight it out, and even worse, leave it up to a judge to decide whose perspective is more accurate.

While many people are hesitant to bring up the subject of a prenup, hopefully you've seen by now why it is so vital, and that the potentially difficult conversation it requires is well worth any temporary discomfort. In Rebecca and Jon's case, a prenup could have helped to prevent the disintegration of their relationship in the first place. Moreover, with a prenup, they could have determined what would happen if they got divorced—dictating that Jon was to be repaid for his investment in Rebecca's tuition, Rebecca would retain her partnership interest, and more.

IF YOU'RE A PARENT

If your child is getting married and his or her spouse-to-be has student loans, you may be considering paying off those loans. Or you may want to buy the lovely couple a car or help them purchase a house. You may even want to furnish that house with some heirloom pieces that have been in your family for decades. But if you do any of that without putting something in writing, and one day those lovebirds get divorced, your ex son- or daughter-in-law will likely end up with a gift you didn't intend to give.

To avoid this obviously undesirable outcome, if you pay off debt or give money or items that you'd want to be returned to you or your child in the case of divorce, then documentation, either by way of a prenup or a loan agreement, is a must. That way, you have the opportunity to pursue repayment.

So, if you intend to give your child money to buy a home after she gets married, it should be written right into the prenup that in the event of divorce, the money would be repaid either to you or your child. If you decide to pay off your daughter-in-law's student debt, be specific that it's a loan, and have her sign a loan document that legally obligates her to repay you. Without anything in writing, it's just a gift, and you don't have a leg to stand on to get it back.

While you may be happy to give a gift to your son- or daughter-in law if all goes swimmingly, you still need to create a legitimate loan document in case it doesn't. Otherwise, he or she could easily say it was a gift that was never expected to be paid back and you would have a difficult, if not impossible, time proving otherwise in court.

Consider the following common circumstances that arise when families combine, as well as how to proceed in order to protect your investment:

Paying for Your Grandchild's Schooling

Many grandparents set up a 529 plan to help pay for their grand-children's tuition. If you're going to do this, think about putting the account in your name, which gives you complete control of the funds. If you put it in your daughter's name and she gets divorced, her ex is going to want that 529 plan to be used to cover college *before* his contribution is calculated. Should you decide to go this route—and give your daughter full control—put it in writing that if she and her husband divorce, the 529 plan is only to be used toward your daughter's portion of tuition.

It is also important to note that when grandparents pay for their grandchildren's expenses, such as private school tuition, they're establishing a precedent of gifting to their children and grandchildren. As such, you could wind up facing an argument that because you've always contributed in such a way, you have to continue to pay for those expenses if your child gets divorced, letting his or her ex-spouse off the hook. You don't want to have to hire a lawyer—and spend money on legal fees—to defend your generosity. Having a prenup or loan documentation can prevent that from happening.

Buying a Home for Your Child

Let's say your daughter asks for $500,000 so she and your future son-in-law can purchase their dream home. If you simply give her the money and she and your son-in-law buy the home and put it in joint names, in most states, he would be entitled to a percentage (maybe even 50 percent) of its value if they get divorced. If they break up, and your intent was to give your now-ex son-in-law—the man who broke your daughter's heart—a gift of $250,000, congratulations—you've just accomplished that. However, if it seems more reasonable to get (or have your daughter get) the entire $500,000 back if they divorce, you can accomplish that by either:

1. Having your daughter and son-in-law both sign a loan document indicating that the $500,000 was a loan requiring full repayment. If the couple stays together, you may never pursue loan repayment—but it will be up to you, not the court; and/or

2. Insisting that the couple sign a prenuptial agreement that clearly states that any money you give to them to purchase assets would be repaid to you or your daughter if they get divorced.

Gifting Engagement Rings

In most states, engagement rings are considered conditional gifts. The condition is, of course, marriage—if the marriage doesn't happen, you get the ring back. But once the couple has said their "I do's," it's a done deal: the ring belongs to the recipient forever, unless you make sure that there is a prenup that states you'll get it back if the couple divorces.

If you're a parent with an engagement ring you'd like to pass on, give it to your daughter, not your son. Should your son propose with it, you risk losing your diamond if he and your daughter-in-law divorce. But when your daughter has it, it remains hers in any circumstance.

Weddings

You're not going to get the money back for the cost of a wedding—regardless of how long the relationship lasts. Keep that in mind if you're considering dropping many thousands of dollars on your future daughter-in-law's fairytale wedding dress.

Just as spouses-to-be feel stressed about broaching some of these tricky subjects, parents worry about provoking animosity by addressing these matters with their kids. But you can't be afraid to bring them up: if you're giving your child the benefit of a debt-free relationship, a wonderful home, or anything else of value—experiences and items he or she wouldn't be able to afford without you—it needs to be done on your terms.

The bottom line? Life is uncertain. While it is wonderful to support the people you love, protecting your investment should also be a priority. Since you can't predict the future, building in financial fail-safes—and knowing just what you're getting yourself into—should be part of the process.

Next, we'll discuss another big marital decision: should one spouse stop working and stay at home?

CHAPTER SIX

SHOULD YOU LET YOUR
SPOUSE STOP WORKING?

First of all, whether or not your spouse stops working may not be up to you! I've seen it happen: as soon as the thank-you notes for the wedding gifts have gone out, one spouse decides that he or she is no longer going to work and expects to be supported by the other. I've seen couples get divorced over this very issue. Is it right? Is it fair?

It's not for me to say what's acceptable to you. But it is very important that you tell your spouse-to-be what you find acceptable— and what you don't! This is another topic that rarely gets discussed before marriage, although it has a tremendous impact on your life in multiple ways, including the very strong feelings a disparity in professional and household responsibilities evoke. Perhaps you're hesitant to talk about it because you're afraid of how your spouse might react, or you just assume you're on the same page. I can assure you it's a conversation you want to have now; as we've seen, avoiding any of these topics or hiding your true feelings almost always hurts more in the end.

Even if you're all for your spouse staying home while you work, you have to consider the long-term effects of that decision. The choices you make today about how the two of you structure your financial life have ramifications that will last into old age. For instance, if the working spouse loses his job or becomes disabled three decades into his career—during which time his wife has been home, her employability having dwindled with each passing year— what will they do now? Alternatively, if the working spouse remains gainfully employed and the marriage doesn't work out, he or she will have to pay spousal support for decades, or even forever.

Whether you're determined to remain a two-income household or desperate to be home to raise your children, here are some things to think about and discuss *as a couple* before making this significant decision:

The Cost of Childcare

Childcare can be tremendously expensive. If one spouse will find him or herself breaking even when they factor in the cost of care—or even paying more than they make to a nanny or daycare facility—staying home may be the most cost-efficient option. But while you may find this route to be cost-effective, there are other considerations to keep in mind.

The Four D's: Disability, Disaster, Divorce, and Death

What if your spouse becomes disabled? What if a disaster occurs? What if your husband or wife loses his or her well-paying job? What if he or she divorces you? What if he or she dies? Nothing is guaranteed in life, and if you're a one-paycheck family, you're putting yourself at risk.

Another Avenue for Resentment

There is a lot of potential for resentments to build when one spouse is gainfully employed, and the other is not. The working spouse may think he is doing more for the partnership because he endures the daily grind of going to work—suffering through a commute, managing conflict with his boss, and shouldering the immense pressure that both job-driven deadlines and being the sole provider entail. When he comes home, and the house is a mess or dinner isn't ready, he may feel like his spouse is taking advantage.

Simultaneously, the spouse at home cares for the children 24/7 and engages in the daily drudgery of maintaining their lives. If her husband comes home and completely disengages after she's been with the kids all day—refusing to interact with them or even wash a dish—she may quickly reach the end of her rope.

Ego

A person's profession is very tightly tied to his or her ego. When giving up a career, people frequently stop feeling good about themselves. Even if a stay-at-home spouse has found the experience to be completely fulfilling, he may find that once the kids are grown and don't need him as much, he may feel bored or worthless—especially if he has been out of the workforce for a long time and faces significant barriers to reenter it.

DO YOU THINK WHAT YOUR SPOUSE DOES IS WORTH AS MUCH AS WHAT YOU DO?

Few gainfully employed people think working inside the home raising children is of equal value to work done outside the home. Often, the partner with a formal job feels superior to the one who shoulders the weight of child rearing and other domestic responsibilities. He believes that because he is bringing home a paycheck, his spouse should be ever so grateful to him. This issue also arises when there's a significant disparity between incomes—say, one spouse makes $350,000 a year while the other brings in just $40,000, even though both spouses view themselves as working equally as hard.

Yet, if you get divorced—depending on the state you're in, the person who hasn't made an equal financial contribution is still going to get an equal portion of assets, as well as spousal support. This should be a big part of the equation when you are deciding whether one party should stop working. Spousal support is a key factor here, so let's touch briefly on how it works.

SPOUSAL SUPPORT

The purpose of spousal support is to limit the financial impact of divorce on a spouse who is not working or who is earning significantly less than his or her partner, acknowledging that the non-earning or low-earning spouse contributed to the marriage by supporting the family in other ways. It is also meant to help maintain the standard of living the low- or non-earning spouse had during the marriage.

When determining spousal support, the courts take into account a variety of factors such as:

- Age

- Mental and physical health

- Assets and liabilities

- Length of time necessary for the low- or non-earning individual to become self-sufficient

- Standard of living during the marriage

- The ability of one spouse to support the other and still cover his or her own expenses

People often feel a sense of pride in the fact that they make enough money that their spouses "don't have to work." But if you are married to someone who's not working during the marriage and he or she has been out of the workforce for a significant amount of time, should you get divorced, the reality is—unless you live in a state that doesn't have spousal support—you're going to wind up paying it, and often for a long time.

In deciding that your spouse will stop working, you are also deciding, perhaps not consciously, that you are willing to pay support if you get divorced.

No one wants to pay spousal support, and no one paying spousal support thinks they are paying too little. I've never heard anyone say they were happy to do it because their spouse made their life so much easier, and it was so much better for their kids to have a parent at home—whether or not that was actually the case.

Meanwhile, the stay-at-home spouse faces issues of his or her own. No one wants to be financially dependent, and no one receiving spousal support thinks they are getting too much. Whether someone receives spousal support—as well as the amount she receives and for how long—depends a lot on the number of years she has been out of work and what has happened to her skillset. If you decide you will stop working, you are also deciding (again, perhaps not consciously), to potentially relinquish your career and financial independence. The choice to stay at home is yours to make, but don't do it with a blind eye to the consequences.

Unless you are a divorce attorney, it is not likely that you know the divorce laws in your state. One of the many great things about entering into a prenup is the corresponding education you receive on what those laws are and how they will affect you, depending on the decisions you make.

Before and during marriage, couples make important life decisions without considering how the laws will affect them if they wind up getting divorced. So many of my clients lament that they would have made different choices had they known how the law would treat those decisions when their marriages ended. Choosing whether to be gainfully employed during the marriage is a classic example. Would you agree to quit your job if it meant you'd have no means of supporting yourself in the event of a divorce? Would you agree to your spouse quitting his or her job if it meant you would have to pay spousal support for the rest of your life?

My client Greg wishes he'd known the law regarding spousal support when he quit his boring desk job to pursue his dream of being a musician: he received only a nominal amount of spousal support in his divorce and found himself unable to secure a lucrative position after having been out of the workforce for a number of years.

Another client, Carolyn, wishes she had not permitted her husband, Joe, to quit his job and stay home with their children. Now she not only pays spousal support to Joe but has also lost primary custody of their children due to her long work hours.

If Greg and Carolyn had gotten prenups, they would have discussed these possible life decisions and what they would mean if they got divorced. If Greg and Carolyn had been aware of the legal consequences of their choices upon divorce, perhaps they would have acted differently during their marriages.

CONSIDER THESE ADDITIONAL SCENARIOS:

Margot and Zach

Margot and Zach have been married for nine years and have two children, ages six and eight. Margot is a doctor who stopped working after the birth of her first child. Zach is an engineer and earns $150,000 per year. While Margot being an at-home mom was acceptable to Zach while they were married, now that they are getting divorced, Zach is claiming he should not have to pay spousal support since, with both kids in school, Margot can easily return to her career as a doctor and earn as much, if not more, than he can.

Since Margot is young and healthy, has only been out of her field for eight years, and can potentially earn as much as Zach does, it is likely she will either get no spousal support at all or only receive a small amount for a short period of time.

Margot is claiming she needs spousal support because she must acquire new training to keep up with the advances in medicine that have occurred over the last eight years and cannot get a job overnight—nor one that pays her $150,000. Who "wins" in this scenario?

Neither Margot nor Zach envisioned their current situation when they decided Margot would stop working. Had they discussed it beforehand, they could have had drafted a written agreement that protected each of their interests.

Lisa and Brian

Lisa and Brian have been married for twenty-seven years and have grown children. Lisa is forty-nine and Brian is fifty years old. Brian gave up his construction job to be an at-home dad when their first child was born twenty-five years ago. Lisa continued to work as a nurse with an annual salary of $120,000.

Lisa and Brian are divorcing and Brian is seeking spousal support from his wife due to his inability to return to a career in construction at his advanced age.[1] Lisa's position is that, although Brian might not be able to get a job as a construction worker, he is healthy and capable of getting a job in another field (perhaps not earning as much as $120,000 per year) to offset the amount of spousal support Lisa must pay him. Will the court decide that Brian will receive less spousal support due to his ability to earn? Or will it rule that he has been out of work for too long and is at an age where any employment is unlikely, entitling him to the maximum amount of spousal support?

Even if the court rules in Brian's favor, if Lisa retires and spousal support ends, how will Brian support himself?

I doubt Brian and Lisa would make the same decisions if they knew what the end results would be. It is one thing to make things work financially when living under one roof in an intact marriage, and quite another when that marriage dissolves.

Here is yet another area where planning and conversations make the difference. If becoming a one-income household is what you choose to do—as a couple, and hopefully with the assistance of a financial advisor—you need to guard against outcomes that can be detrimental to your financial health or cause resentments to build.

---

[1] It's important to note that the courts don't discriminate based on gender. More and more, women are becoming the family breadwinners, and they are no less susceptible to spousal support. If you're the financially supporting spouse, you're on the hook. Women who serve as the primary financial providers also risk losing custody of their children or having to share custody equally if they are not the primary caregivers.

If you decide as a couple that once a child is born, one spouse won't work, maybe you also agree that the arrangement is not forever—that when the kids start school, he or she also finds a job. It's also important to discuss what happens if the financial burden that arises from a sole income becomes untenable. If it's putting a financial strain on you as a couple, tensions and finger-pointing are likely to arise, and it may be time to pursue a different route. No matter what, talk about any discomfort you have with the situation. And go to couples' counseling the minute resentments or feelings of inequity appear.

CHAPTER SEVEN

WHAT HAPPENS TO AN INHERITANCE IF A MARRIAGE DOESN'T LAST?

I t's common to be very protective of an inheritance, and reasonably so. Millennials are slated to be the first generation less prosperous than their parents, so inheritances may play a significant role in your future—or your children's. And as with many of the subjects we've discussed here, the way inherited assets are handled during a marriage affects how they are divided in the event of divorce.

If you'll be receiving or bequeathing an inheritance, it's important to understand how marriage and divorce can affect the way it is distributed. For instance, in many states, as long as inheritances are not commingled with marital property, they are not subject to be divided with a spouse in the event of divorce. However, the interest on the inheritance may be considered income for the purpose of support. Is that something you're entirely comfortable with? If you answered "no," you're not alone.

In this chapter, we'll look at the considerations involving inheritances—which vary from state to state—and discuss the factors you need to think about if there is a bequest in your future.

IF YOU'LL BE RECEIVING AN INHERITANCE

While everything is snuggles and smooches now, if something does go wrong over the course of your marriage and you get divorced, chances are you're not going to be interested in giving a portion of your inheritance to your ex. It's likely that the people leaving you their assets wouldn't be too thrilled either. If you want to make sure your inheritance remains yours, you must take appropriate measures. While prenups of course reign supreme in terms of determining what happens to an inheritance, there are other measures you can take to protect it:

Keep It Separate

In states where inheritances are considered marital assets, there's nothing you can do to shield those funds, short of a prenup. But if your state *does* consider inheritances to be individual property, it's crucial to keep that money completely separate from anything shared with your spouse: once it's been commingled, it becomes a marital asset, and in the event of divorce, it will be treated as if you gifted him or her a portion of those funds. Even if you only use the interest from an inherited or gifted asset, the other party may be able to argue that those dollars were income for the marital lifestyle. Don't add inherited funds to money you saved during your marriage; don't put them in a joint bank account; don't use them to buy a house and put that house in both your names.

Take the case of my client, Sam, whose wife, Keara, was divorcing him to be with her high school sweetheart less than a year after Sam had used his inherited money to pay off the couple's credit card debt. Sam was quite unhappy when I told him he could not seek reimbursement of his inheritance from Keara because he had spent it.

Even worse, Sam was not entitled to any part of Keara's inheritance because—unlike Sam—she had put hers in a bank account in her own name and never touched it. Sam lamented that if he had known the law regarding inheritances, he would have done things differently.

Don't Yield to Emotional Blackmail or Threats

If you are married, keeping an inheritance to yourself is the way to go, especially if you don't have a prenup. However, this decision can become a source of strife in many relationships. You may face pressure from your partner: your husband may claim that, since he's had to put up with your mother for all these years, it's only fair that you share some of her money with him. Your wife may insist that since you got so much money from your grandparents, you should use it to pay for your child's college tuition. Or she may claim that you don't love her if you don't put the house or car you purchased with your inherited money in both of your names.

Sometimes, threats come next; I've heard about fiancés, husbands, and wives threatening to withhold sex, quit their jobs, or do any of a thousand other crazy things because they disagree with their partners' thinking about how to handle an inheritance. If you give in to these threats, you will be very unhappy down the line when your spouse gets a portion (maybe even 50 percent) of what was intended just for you. If you are not married and know you will be receiving an inheritance in the future, it is essential that you seek your fiancé's agreement to enter into a prenup that protects it under all circumstances. If your fiancé refuses and threatens not to marry you if you won't share your inheritance, take a moment to consider what we discussed in chapter 4: how will this kind of behavior affect you over the course of your marriage? If this is a warning of what's to come, it may be a good time to get out while you still can.

IF YOU'LL BE BEQUEATHING ASSETS

Perhaps the shoe is on the other foot, and you want to ensure your child gets to keep the bequest that you intend for him or her. There are a variety of actions you can take to help your child preserve his or her inheritance, depending on your situation:

If Your Child Is Getting Married

If your child is engaged, make sure she has a prenup stating that anything she inherits solely belongs to her and is not subject to division if she and her future husband divorce. You should also instruct her to protect her inheritance by not commingling it with marital assets after she and her husband tie the knot.

If you want to add an extra level of protection to your bequest, you can put it into a trust. With a trust, *you* set the terms that determine whether and when a spouse gets to share those funds. This may be a particularly good choice if your future son- or daughter-in-law won't agree to a prenup, or if your child is already married. When deciding whether to establish a trust, it is also advisable to have a heart to heart with your child: tell him you can either put the inheritance into a trust and keep full control or rely on him not to commingle it so it stays in the family. Not all trusts offer the kind of protection you might be looking for, so be sure to consult with an attorney who specializes in trusts and estates.

When You're Marrying with Children

Inheritances are an especially important subject for those who already have children and are marrying for a second or third time. In fact, this particular circumstance was what popularized prenuptial agreements to begin with (though, as you've hopefully seen by now, they're equally important the first time around). You may want to ensure that some or all of your wealth is earmarked for your children, as opposed to the majority of it going to your spouse—which could be the case if you don't make your intentions clear. Again, a prenup can accomplish this for you, as can clever trust and estate planning.

Don't Let the State Decide

If you don't take measures to clearly document your wishes, state laws will dictate how your estate is divided. However, a prenup takes precedence. If you'd rather have your assets go to your children than to your new spouse after your death, a prenup is essential.

A prenup can delineate the distribution of your assets in whatever manner you see fit. For instance, the prenup may state that you will set up a trust containing a certain amount of money for your spouse. If you predecease her, your spouse will be able to live off the income from the trust while she is alive, and when she dies, the principal will go to your children. By appointing an independent trustee, you can essentially control the trust from beyond the grave, ensuring that your children get everything in the end.

To preserve funds for your kids, your prenup should state that if you predecease your spouse, he or she waives his or her right to take from your estate and that you will determine in your will what your spouse will receive. While a prenup is only drafted once, your will can be updated as frequently as you like, allowing you more control over how your assets are distributed.

If you don't plan to leave your spouse an inheritance, you may want to stipulate in your prenup that you will maintain a life insurance policy naming her as the beneficiary, thereby ensuring she receives financial support if you predecease her. This is an especially good choice if you are young and healthy, as a good life insurance policy will be extremely inexpensive.

Your prenup can also determine what happens to your home upon your death. The prenup may indicate that if you—the homeowner—die first, your spouse can continue living in the home until he or she dies, at which point your children inherit the property (though this wouldn't work well if your spouse is around the same age as your adult children, which is sometimes the case).

CASE IN POINT

I recently prepared a prenuptial agreement for a seventy-two-year-old man, Jack, who was marrying a sixty-year-old woman, Moira. Jack and Moira had dated for fifteen years, and they each had adult children from prior marriages. While Moira had some assets, they paled in comparison to Jack's substantial net worth. Jack wanted to protect his assets for his children, but given their long-term relationship, he also wanted to make sure Moira was taken care of financially in the event that he predeceased her.

We were able to accomplish this by executing a prenuptial agreement that provided for Moira to receive a percentage of Jack's estate outright, and to receive support throughout her lifetime through a trust—which we prepared with the help of a trust and estate attorney. Through this process, Jack ensured Moira's financial needs would be covered, and there would still be plenty left for his children.

Maintaining control over an inheritance requires you to have tough conversations and plan accordingly. Death is inevitable, and failing to document your wishes properly can create more pain for your loved ones during an already difficult time. Voicing your intentions—and taking steps to ensure they are honored—may cause some distress, but you can take comfort in the fact that your loved ones will get what you want them to have, no matter what.

CHAPTER EIGHT

MINDING YOUR OWN BUSINESS: HOW MUCH DOES A SPOUSE GET IN A SPLIT?

Maybe you own a .business, or you're part of a family business—or your parents are going to leave you theirs—and you're curious about how your upcoming marriage could affect your ownership stake. Or perhaps you are a parent, and you plan on passing your generations-old firm down to your newly engaged child. Are you aware that a spouse—yours or your child's—could be entitled to up to half the value of your family operation in a divorce?

Once again, if there is no prenup in place, you may have to give up a huge chunk of the value of your business in a divorce. While this kind of thinking is not the stuff of love songs, writing a great big check to your former spouse—or the person who broke your child's heart—would probably have you singing a different tune! (And don't tell me this could never happen in your family. That's what *everybody* thinks.)

ASSET DISTRIBUTION

Before we delve into the ins and outs of dividing up the value of a business in the case of divorce, we have to talk about asset distribution. This applies to all assets and liabilities, not just to family businesses.

Few people realize that, without a prenup, there is little to no way to fully protect the assets they acquire during marriage, even if they obtain them with premarital money or keep them in their own names—an issue we touched on in the previous chapter. Anything they own that is acquired during the marriage via any route is potentially subject to be divided in the case of divorce.

The way it is distributed depends on the state. In community property states, all property acquired over the course of a marriage is divvied up equally in the case of a divorce, while in the others, courts allocate assets using a method called "equitable distribution."

It's crucial to note that "equitable" does not necessarily mean "equal," and if you don't have a prenup, you're subject to the courts' conception of what's fair when it comes to what you get. In general, the courts will use the following factors to determine equitable distribution:

- how long you've been married

- your age and your physical and mental health

- the standard of living you established during the marriage

- your respective contributions to the amount or value of the marital property, which includes the support and services provided by the party who served as homemaker (if it's relevant)

- whether the person who has physical custody of a child needs to own or occupy the marital residence and use or own particular household effects.

Remember, if you don't have a prenup, the law of the state in which you reside when you file for divorce applies; you should always check with a local lawyer to learn about the laws specific to your state.

Now that we've established how equitable distribution works, you can imagine its potential effect on your business and understand why it's so important to prepare accordingly. If a business will be a factor in your or your child's impending nuptials, there are some things to keep in mind.

IF YOU'RE GETTING MARRIED AND YOU HAVE A BUSINESS

If you own your own business, or you're part of a family business, you likely understand how much is at stake when it comes to your livelihood—plus the additional layer of complications that can arise when partners or relatives are involved. As a result of this complex arrangement, stress, feelings of inequality, and lack of respect can bubble up and fuel marital issues. While that doesn't necessarily mean you're more likely to get divorced, it's necessary to know where you stand—and what you stand to lose—from the outset.

Those who have inherited or are set to inherit a family business are primary candidates for prenuptial agreements because a prenup is the only way to truly preserve its value. If you own your own business, the same considerations apply: your spouse could be entitled to part of the value of your business or any increase in value that occurs over the course of your marriage. Thus, you need to take the same precautions. Even if you're just *thinking* about starting your own business, a prenup can protect you by stating that your spouse waives the right to the value of any future businesses.

This is especially imperative because if you do break up, you're at risk of having a very expensive divorce. Why? You'll be splitting the *value* of the business—rather than the business itself—with your spouse. To determine exactly how much that is, you'll need to hire a forensic accountant, whose fees could be even more than your lawyer's! With one accountant for you, one for your spouse, and potentially a third to settle the score if the first two don't agree, you could easily be looking at substantially more in additional fees—not to mention the disruption of business operations and the invasion of privacy inherent in the process as the forensic accountant looks into your books, records, tax returns, and more.

IF YOUR SPOUSE-TO-BE HAS A FAMILY BUSINESS

If you're marrying someone with a family business, make sure you understand his or her stake in it—and what that could mean for the family *you're* establishing.

Say your husband has worked at his family's company for twenty years of your marriage and never received any ownership interest—all while keeping long hours for little pay and continuing to invest in the business based on his parents' promise that "someday this will all be yours." You've contributed, too, working full time in a different industry to make up for his paltry salary and spending weekends with the in-laws at the office. You even helped the business grow, lending your expertise to launch marketing campaigns that brought in throngs of new customers over the years.

Despite all of those years of effort, if you eventually get divorced, you won't get anything from that business—no matter how successful it is or how much you did to increase its value. If your husband doesn't have any ownership interest, there's nothing to get.

On the other hand, if your spouse does own a business, or if your spouse-to-be intends to start one in the future, don't sign away your interest without getting anything in return.

Even if you love your future in-laws and they seem to love you back, don't assume they'll be generous when it comes to sharing a portion of their company or treating you fairly if you agree to give up your interest. People treat their businesses like children, and there's nothing like entering into a family with its own enterprise to make you realize your in-laws don't really consider you their kin.

Take the case of my client, Charlie, who "should've known" he was going to have a difficult time with his future wife Jennifer's parents when *they* were the ones to present him with a prenuptial agreement two weeks before the wedding. Jennifer's parents owned a business, and Jennifer worked there and was significantly underpaid. The plan was that Jennifer's parents would gift portions of their business to Jennifer over time so that she would eventually own it all and earn a substantial income.

Under the terms of the prenuptial agreement, Charlie waived spousal support, his rights to any ownership interest in the business that Jennifer acquired during the marriage, *and* any growth in the value of the business due to Jennifer's work there.

Pressured by his future in-laws, Charlie signed the prenup against my advice and married Jennifer. During the marriage, Charlie used all of his income to support the family and acquire assets—which he placed in both his and Jennifer's names. Jennifer continued to work for low wages in her family's business, and the couple struggled financially as a result.

They began to argue almost daily—Charlie wanted Jennifer to ask her parents for fair pay. Jennifer refused, insisting it was okay that they gave her so little because she would one day own the company and earn a substantial income. This was true; by the time Charlie showed up in my office, Jennifer had been gifted a 50 percent ownership interest in the business. However, their relationship had reached a breaking point.

I was in the unfortunate position of giving Charlie the bad news that, because he'd signed the prenup—in which he waived spousal support and any interest in the business—he would receive neither in their divorce.

Meanwhile, Jennifer would keep her now-substantial income, retain her ownership interest in the business, not have to pay spousal support, *and* receive half of the assets Charlie had worked to acquire during the marriage. In this case, signing the one-sided prenuptial agreement forced upon him by his in-laws left Charlie in a worse position than if there had been no prenup at all.

IF YOU'RE GIFTING OR LEAVING A BUSINESS TO YOUR CHILD

If you gift or bequeath a business to your child, your son- or daughter-in-law could be entitled to share in the value of the business or the increase in its value during the marriage. What's worse, if you live in a state where gifts or inheritances from third parties are considered marital assets, your business could suddenly become your ex-daughter-in-law's business.

The only way to get around this, as you may have already guessed, is to have your child enter into a prenup stating that when he or she receives the business from you, his or her spouse waives the right to any value in the business, even if your child's work efforts increase its value.

CASE IN POINT

This particular situation was an important consideration for my client Mr. Casey, who owns a business and wants to gift it to his son, Jim. Jim is getting married, and Mr. Casey was concerned that the business—or its potential increase in value during Jim's marriage—would be an asset to which Joan, Jim's fiancée, would be entitled in the event that they divorced.

I advised Mr. Casey that a prenuptial agreement executed by Jim and Joan could eliminate the possibility of Joan getting any part of it. But Mr. Casey questioned whether it would be fair for Joan to get nothing if she ended up working in the business and/or supporting Jim as he contributed to the company's growth.

I suggested to Mr. Casey that the couple's prenup could specify that Joan gets a certain amount of money or additional spousal support in exchange for her "share of the business." Or it could include a sunset clause stating that after a certain number of years of marriage, the prenuptial agreement would expire. He chose the first option, and Jim and Joan agreed to sign a prenuptial agreement with those terms.

Thanks to his son's prenup, Mr. Casey was able to gift his business to Jim without the worry that Joan could disrupt or deplete the business if she and Jim divorced.

What if your child's future spouse won't agree to a prenup? As a parent, you may also have the option of putting business interests in a trust, depending on your state's laws. Doing so gives you control, enabling you to guard against your child's spouse being able to access its value. While this may limit your child's ability to manage the business as he or she sees fit, it could be a worthwhile course of action if you don't have another option. Be sure to consult with a trust and estate attorney to make sure the trust is actually accomplishing your goals.

THE BOTTOM LINE

The heart of the matter is this: no one can predict the future, so protection is essential. When you have a family business—or you depend on one for your household income—there is much to be lost if and when a marriage sours.

Consider the steps you'd take to protect your share of a company if your partners weren't tied to you by blood or matrimony, and make sure you're preserving your stake here, too. Understand the laws in your state and how they could apply to your situation. Bolstered by that knowledge, you can act accordingly, creating a prenup, agreement, and/or trust that provides the fail-safe support you need.

CHAPTER NINE

IF YOU'RE FIGHTING ABOUT MONEY, YOU'RE REALLY FIGHTING ABOUT WHO'S THE BOSS

F ast forward to a handful of years from now: vows have been exchanged, the cake has been cut, checks cashed, registry appliances put to use in a flurry of excitement and smoothies, and then forgotten in the back of your pantry. By now, reality has set in, and you have a home together, and maybe even a couple of kids. With the complications of life and all of its tedious necessities—work, taxes, in-laws, parent-teacher conferences—you may find that, though you willingly agreed to "for better, for worse," your days are plagued by more of the latter.

Whereas your husband's tendency to talk in his sleep or your wife's high-pitched laugh seemed truly adorable while you were dating, his or her every move has started to drive you crazy—and not with blinding passion. Soon, you find yourself entangled in arguments large and small, and the beautiful life you've built together feels more like a bear trap. So, what happened?

Over years of long commutes, thousands of loads of laundry, and weekends spent at hockey games and piano recitals, couples find themselves short on the time and energy they used to invest in their relationship. They forget that marriage is a partnership.

If they were in business together, they wouldn't dare to make decisions without consulting each other, but in the context of marriage, doing so becomes routine. Each person takes on certain roles and ceases to check in with his or her spouse. Over time, they fail to remember that they weren't forced into the particular slate of responsibilities they've accepted, and each party is sure he or she is being taken advantage of by the other. Tensions rise, and things begin to fall apart because spouses no longer feel like equals.

MONEY MATTERS

Of course, everyone wants to be treated equally. When it feels as if that's not happening, many disputes manifest in the form of money, the ultimate equalizer. You may find that your arguments are about finances more than anything else: who's spending what and how much, or the causes and priorities that deserve your hard-earned cash. Psychologists will tell you that those arguments are actually battles over power and control in a relationship. In other words, you may be fighting over a credit card bill or whether to send your kid to private school, but in reality, the real clash has to do with who's the "boss" in the relationship.

A husband will tell me his wife spends money like it's water, though he's the only one who earns it. Meanwhile, she'll complain that he insists on maintaining complete control over their finances and disregards her opinions and her needs, even though it's *her* efforts at home that allow him to work the eighty-hour weeks necessary to bring home that big paycheck. While they may have agreed on this arrangement at the outset of their relationship—perhaps they even determined that they'd spend as much as she'd make on a nanny and a housekeeper if she were to work—that analysis gets lost in the sauce when they're both feeling underappreciated and undervalued.

If you feel as if you aren't on equal footing with your spouse, it's likely because you believe he or she has more power than you do. Dollars, how they're distributed, and how they're spent are often the easiest way to voice this discomfort. And, unfortunately, money is power—there's no way around it.

Being proactive about your relationship—and your finances—is crucial to the ultimate success of your relationship.

FIND FINANCIAL HARMONY

One of the best ways to avoid some marital conflict is to find someone with financial values that mirror your own. If you can agree on the big picture, you'll face fewer snags than couples with completely divergent spending philosophies.

Ideally, you both believe it's worth it to put off a decade of extravagant vacations with the goal of buying a beach house, or that sending your kids to college trumps spending an extra $200,000 on your dream home. If you've discovered that your values don't completely align, be prepared to find common ground. Your prenuptial agreement is the perfect place to document any compromises. Take your agreed-upon goals and interests into account and put into writing your responsibilities to each other and to ensuring your financial future.

Whether or not you're completely compatible financially, check in frequently to ensure you're on the same page and course-correct if you're not. Change is just part of life. You may start out staying at home, but what happens if your spouse loses his or her job? If your marriage is truly a partnership, you need to be prepared to step up.

KNOW THAT IGNORANCE IS NOT BLISS

Some couples decide together that one spouse will handle all the money matters. Other spouses find themselves in a situation in which one partner insists on taking it all on, and the other gives up control just to keep the peace. If you are willing to give up full financial control, be ready to deal with the consequences. In addition to being owed a portion of the marital assets in the case of divorce, you're also responsible for marital debt. Maybe you willingly leave the bills and investment decisions to your wife, but what happens when something goes awry, and you learn she put a year's worth of expensive lunches on a credit card you didn't know you had, or that she failed to report a large portion of income on your tax return? Ignorance doesn't make you any less accountable.

Even if your prenup states that your spouse is assuming full responsibility for your finances and any corresponding issues, it's not foolproof; third parties like the IRS and credit card companies are not subject to your contract.

Rather than banking on ignorance, I suggest you consider why you're willing to give up so much control, and how that decision may affect you down the line.

DON'T IGNORE THE SIGNS

As we discussed in chapter 4, you should never have to say, "I should have known," when it comes to your marriage; you can uncover the answers through a series of thorough questions and keen observations.

If you've been ignoring any uncomfortable interactions regarding money—indications that the dreamboat to whom you plan to say "I do" has some control issues—and go ahead with your marriage anyway, those issues are probably going to resurface.

Say, for instance, your future husband insists that you stay home to take care of your children once they're born. Perhaps you get the sense that the primary reason for his persistence is not because he thinks you'll provide your babies with the best possible care, but because he wants to keep close tabs on you or simply feed his ego—bragging about his impressive earnings to family and friends: "My wife doesn't have to work." When those children are old enough, you may find that your husband has painted them a somewhat disturbing picture of your household roles and responsibilities, diminishing your contributions and worth. Suddenly, you're facing pushback from your kids, something along the lines of, "Mom, I don't have to listen to you because you don't do anything." Their father has convinced them that he is the provider and you're just there for show. Now what?

If the signs continue to rack up as you're drafting your prenup, or even after you're married, tune in and consider what you're willing to accept. Money dictates so much of our lives, and difficult decisions only get harder over time.

TALK AND LISTEN

I have never spoken with a married couple in which each party feels completely equal to his or her spouse. However, those with the strongest relationships talk about their respective positions. They share their feelings about their jobs and responsibilities, how hard they are, and why they feel underappreciated at times.

One person is not afraid to tell the other, "I know you don't think it's a lot of work to be at home all day, but let me explain to you why it is. While you were out to lunch with your clients, I didn't have time to eat anything because I was tending to two sick kids." Hopefully, the other spouse listens and adjusts his or her perspective accordingly.

Maintaining a happy, healthy, and functioning relationship is not just about being open and honest *before* you get married; it's about being open and honest *while* you're married. Doing so requires that you not keep things that are bothering you to yourself—especially when it comes to financial values, spending habits, or lack of respect. You are bound to find that your spouse has a different set of grievances. A strong understanding of your spouse's struggles breeds compassion and benefits your union. I urge you to speak up before you're too frustrated to care about where he or she is coming from.

If you can't reach a consensus on your own, this is where a third party—someone who isn't partial to a particular side—should weigh in.

WHEN TO FIND A THIRD-PARTY EXPERT

If you can't find common ground or reconcile those feelings of inequality before or during your marriage, don't be afraid to seek support sooner rather than later. We rely on third parties for help all the time when we don't know how to fix things in our lives—a mechanic for a broken exhaust pipe, a dentist for a chipped tooth, a dog trainer for a rambunctious puppy that can't quite grasp the meaning of "sit." Too often we hesitate to get expert help for our relationships, especially once we've said, "I do." But anything of value requires some level of maintenance.

The time to seek help is not when things are already falling apart; you should reach out at the first sign of an issue. Acquiring third-party support when things aren't dire means you'll have the guidance you need to handle the tougher situations that will inevitably come up over the course of your life together.

As we established in chapter 3, sometimes a financial advisor can be more therapeutic than a relationship counselor. If all of your marital tensions are tainted green—and you find yourselves constantly arguing about who spends how much and on what—a financial advisor can set you straight. He or she will review your goals and interests and help you devise a plan for saving, spending, and investing. If you're not completely aligned when it comes to financial values, this might mean choosing a strategy that honors the interests of both parties, especially if one of you insists on saving every penny while the other is considering building a second closet just for shoes.

If you agree to heed a financial advisor's advice, arguments about money should soon dissipate—or at least focus on the root of the issues you're having. Saving toward common goals may also help you remember that you're in this thing together and assuage some of the friction. Plus, it's much harder to argue with your significant other in someone else's office than it is when you're sitting at your kitchen table.

DON'T LET YOUR MARRIAGE GO TO SEED

If you're not fighting about money—or anything else, for that matter—it may be time to check in, too. The lack of tension may not be a sign of success so much as a sign of neglect or apathy. So many people are shocked when they hear their spouse wants a divorce. Even if they've stopped tending to the relationship long ago, it's easy to assume things are still working because, in terms of tasks, the family has become a well-oiled machine. In that sense, it's humming along; the kids make it to hockey practice and dinner's always on the table. But the couple doesn't talk anymore, they don't have sex, and there's very little joy. At the end of the day (or a decade or two), there's not really a marriage left.

This was the case for my client, Todd. Todd had been married to Christina for twenty-five years, but recently Todd decided he'd had enough. Both parties worked full time, but Christina made double Todd's salary. According to Todd, as a result of Christina's earnings, she felt *he* should be responsible for the majority of the household responsibilities. Todd told me he handled all of the laundry, cooking, and their children's weekend schedules while Christina often got drinks with friends on weeknights and spent Saturdays getting her nails done, going to spin class, or splurging on expensive spa treatments.

When I asked if Todd had considered asking Christina to help out more with their kids and the day-to-day chores, he said he had done so for years and that Christina often responded that she handled most of the financial responsibilities, so the least Todd could do was help out more at home. Eventually, Todd stopped asking, and their routine continued for almost a decade. Along the way, their intimacy had all but disappeared. On the rare occasion that they went out alone together, both of them spent the evening staring at their phones.

But when Todd announced he wanted a divorce, Christina was in shock. She said she thought he had been fine with the distribution of labor in their home. She asked if they could go on more dates, offered to take over weekend activities with the kids, and suggested they see a counselor to salvage the relationship, but Todd thought there was nothing left to save.

You fell in love for a reason, but if you don't take steps to remind yourself of it throughout your marriage and make sure the financial and household policies you put in place are benefiting you both, you may find yourself staring into the eyes of a stranger years from now—one you're no longer interested in getting to know.

Divorce is a possibility in everyone's marriage—more than 50 percent of people who marry in the US will learn this the hard way. If you notice issues of inequality cropping up, don't wait to address them until it's too late. Start out with a strong knowledge of the person you're marrying and his or her monetary values; take steps to keep your relationship—and finances—on track; and if you can't resolve something on your own, don't be afraid to get support from a neutral third party while there's still something worth saving.

CHAPTER TEN

OKAY ... NOW YOU CAN
GO GET MARRIED

I acknowledge that this book may have been upsetting to read. Most people go into marriage with stars in their eyes, not dollar signs or divorce statistics. If they anticipate hiring an attorney, they imagine it will be to help them buy a house or create trusts for their children's education—never for divorce.

But there's a reason why more than half of all marriages fail. Actually, there are many reasons, and because you've taken the time to read this book, you are now familiar with the vast majority of them. And since you are aware of the multitude of issues that can crop up when you agree to weather life's challenges as a unit, you also understand just how crucial it is to have a prenuptial agreement, regardless of whether you have or expect to acquire significant wealth.

You know that while raising the subject may be scary at first, a prenup can not only protect you in the case of divorce or death, but also help you learn more about the person you're marrying and better understand your respective priorities. As a binding contract that lays the ground rules for your relationship and what happens in the unfortunate case that it dissolves, your prenup can even prevent a breakup, assisting you in making important decisions and resolving significant disagreements.

You also understand that the validity of this foundational document is essential. Creating a solid, enforceable prenup requires that you check the laws in your state, hire lawyers to represent each of you, so that you both have someone knowledgeable looking out for your interests, and truly agree to the terms of the prenup—not just on paper, but on a fundamental level. The latter also means that one of you isn't pressuring the other into signing under some crazy circumstances (also known as duress).

You've seen the ways in which resentments regarding money have tremendous potential to affect or end your marriage, more—in my experience—than any other issue. We've identified these resentments and covered some steps you can take to end or avoid them, both when they're actually about money and when they're masquerading as finance-related, but really about control.

We've also covered the vital insight-giving experiences to engage in and questions to ask before your wedding day to ensure you know what you're getting yourself into, as well as what to consider when you find something that makes you question your partner's character—like frequent bouts of jealousy, road rage, or a lack of self-control.

These pages have tackled making big purchases as a couple and determining if you should pay a spouse's tuition or debt—including cases where it's your child who's saying "I do"—and gone over the steps you can take to protect a family business or an inheritance, depending on whether you're gifting or gaining one.

You've had the chance to consider the impact on a marriage when one spouse stops working, and what could happen if you end up getting divorced, including the ins and outs of spousal support and asset distribution.

Along the way, I've noted ways to make sure your wishes are carried out by asserting them in your prenup, through a trust, or in estate plans. I've also shown you the consequences of poor planning, faulty contracts, and frustrations left unchecked. Together, we've reviewed real-life cases to see how what we've discussed can play out in divorce court as well.

Having all this in mind will hopefully encourage you to take the proper precautions before marriage and take steps to sustain your union when life attempts to get in the way. The surprise many people feel when their spouse says they want a divorce is often due to the fact that they haven't given much thought to what's been happening in their marriage. If they saw it coming—if they thought about divorce being a possibility—maybe they would have behaved differently or taken action to amend their ways. Unfortunately, by the time they reach my office, it's usually too late.

There are no guarantees in life, but one thing I can promise is that, as unpleasant as these topics may be to think about right now, it's a lot easier to "take your medicine" at this stage of the game than it is to have a marriage crumble years later over a situation that could have been resolved before it began.

The good news is that you don't have to be a depressing divorce statistic. If you are willing to have open and honest discussions about money and marriage before you commit, your relationship has a much better chance of working out than most—and reading this book is a great first step. Running a marriage like a business—with a clear, valid agreement at its outset; an understanding of your goals, hopes, dreams, and desires; and knowledge of what happens if some portion of your plan doesn't work out—can only help your cause, both as individuals and as a couple.

I want the best for you. I want your marriage to succeed. I hope your prenup sits in a drawer and collects dust forever. And I hope that my sharing these thoughts with you will help make your marriage joyous and fulfilling and that it will last "until death do you part."

BEFORE YOU SAY "I DO"

DISCUSSION CHECKLIST

Throughout this book, we've uncovered how what you don't know *can* hurt you and your marriage in a multitude of ways. This checklist will help you cover all the bases as you consider one of the biggest decisions of your life, so you can head into the sunset with confidence. Review the items in each category with your partner and make sure to address any issues that arise *now* to avoid regrets and heartache.

PERSONAL

- ☐ Live together
- ☐ Experience adversity
- ☐ Observe his or her work ethic
- ☐ Discuss your respective goals
- ☐ Determine your shared and separate interests
- ☐ Spend time with friends and their significant others
- ☐ Take vacations together
- ☐ Assess your sexual compatibility—and talk about it if things aren't working
- ☐ Discuss whether you want pets and what kind

- ☐ Get his or her take on education—for you and/or your children
- ☐ Discuss what would happen if one of you were to have a serious health issue or become disabled
- ☐ Learn his or her positions on politics and religion
- ☐ Come to an agreement on household chores
- ☐ Figure out whether your ideal living situations align (location, type of home)
- ☐ Determine whether you have similar values when it comes to cleanliness and organization
- ☐ Talk about your vision for the wedding, and how you'll compromise if you have different ideas

EMOTIONAL

Test for:

- ☐ Anger-management issues
- ☐ Addiction
- ☐ Secrecy
- ☐ Jealousy
- ☐ Infidelity
- ☐ Honesty
- ☐ Trust
- ☐ Clear communication
- ☐ How does your partner deal with forgiveness?
- ☐ Are you both adept at conflict resolution?

If you spot any red flags, head to therapy or relationship counseling *before* embarking on your marriage.

FINANCIAL

*As you prepare for your prenup, disclose
information about your respective:*

- ☐ Incomes
- ☐ Assets
- ☐ Inheritances
- ☐ Businesses
- ☐ Financial support received from other parties
- ☐ Financial obligations to other parties, including spousal and child support
- ☐ Debts, including:
  - ☐ Car
  - ☐ Credit cards
  - ☐ School loans

*Cover the following money-related issues as
well to ensure you're on the same page:*

- ☐ Spending and saving priorities
- ☐ Your desired lifestyle
- ☐ Marital income
- ☐ How you'll cover—and potentially split—the bills
- ☐ Debt tolerance
- ☐ Investment risk tolerance
- ☐ Family wealth
- ☐ Your positions on borrowing and loaning money

Get a handle on your financial future together by:

- ☐ Engaging in estate planning
- ☐ Getting life insurance
- ☐ Setting up a joint savings account

- ☐ Planning for retirement
- ☐ Bringing third-party advisors on board to help you along the way

CAREER

Discuss:

- ☐ How you'll pay for the additional education one or both of you may receive
- ☐ How you'll handle any current or future businesses or business partnerships
- ☐ Your individual work habits
- ☐ How your current and expected compensation compares
- ☐ Whether there is mutual respect and support—and whether you can cultivate it if it's not there
- ☐ What you'd each like your work life to look like after children (if you want to have them)
- ☐ How you'll handle job changes and other professional hurdles and achievements

CHILDREN

If you want to have children together, determine:

- ☐ How many you'd like to have
- ☐ How far apart in age you want them to be
- ☐ Whether you'd consider adoption, IVF, or surrogacy
- ☐ Whether one of you will provide childcare or whether you'll outsource it
- ☐ Your individual responsibilities
- ☐ How you'll handle parental decisions

- ☐ Whether they'll attend private or public school
- ☐ Your opinions on sports and other activities
- ☐ Who will pay for college—and how
- ☐ Your respective values and positions on:
    - ☐ Discipline
    - ☐ Education and military enlistment
    - ☐ Managing health issues and/or special needs
    - ☐ Vaccinations
    - ☐ Gender identity and/or sexuality

If you'll be becoming a step parent, how will you manage parenting and other responsibilities for that child/those children?

FUTURE IN-LAWS (OR OUTLAWS)

You're not just marrying your partner; you're also marrying their family, so make sure to:

- ☐ Learn about your spouse-to-be's relationship with his or her family
- ☐ Get to know your future in-laws yourself and anticipate any tensions that may arise
- ☐ Share any important holidays, traditions, and customs and how you'll celebrate them
- ☐ Discuss what role they will play in your married life and child rearing
- ☐ Determine whether they will provide any financial support to you, your spouse, or your children
- ☐ Discuss your feelings about privacy in your relationship—and how you'll maintain it
- ☐ Disclose any inheritances or gifts, and whether you'll share them or keep them separate

☐ Discuss family businesses, their dynamics, and whether you'll both participate

☐ Talk about how you'll handle any issues that arise with regard to their health and plans for managing their care as they age

☐ Ensure that you are both putting each other first

BEFORE THEY SAY "I DO"

CHECKLIST FOR PARENTS OF CHILDREN GETTING MARRIED

If your child is getting married, his or her partner is also joining your family—and that may require some planning on your part. Consider the following items to ensure that your child and your finances are protected, no matter how the relationship plays out.

PERSONAL

- ☐ Spend time with your future son- or daughter-in-law and anticipate any tensions that may arise
- ☐ Discuss issues that frequently evoke strong feelings, such as religion, politics, and how they'll spend holidays
- ☐ Consider any involvement you may have in their relationship and discuss it with your child
- ☐ Determine whether you are willing to provide childcare or help cover the cost of care for your future grandchildren
- ☐ Check in with the couple about their plans for life insurance, investments, and other factors they may not have considered

FINANCIAL

- ☐ Insist on a prenup
- ☐ If you are giving the couple a family engagement ring, take steps to ensure that you'll get it back if things don't pan out
- ☐ Discuss whether you will contribute to wedding expenses, and how
- ☐ Talk about any assets you plan to gift or leave your child and whether you want his or her spouse to share them

Consider whether you'll contribute to the couple's life together by:

- ☐ Paying off a child-in-law's debt
- ☐ Paying for a child-in-law's education
- ☐ Gifting heirloom jewelry, furniture, or other meaningful items
- ☐ Helping the couple buy a house or car, and/or covering living expenses
- ☐ Ensure that anything you would want back in the case of a divorce is documented as a loan to your child and/or his or her spouse
- ☐ Determine whether you will contribute to a 529 plan or set up other accounts for your grandchildren
- ☐ If you have a family business, discuss its future with your child and your feelings about his or her spouse's participation/ potential to share in its value or profits
- ☐ Engage in your own estate planning and/or create trusts to protect your assets for your child should he or she get divorced

ABOUT THE AUTHOR

As a divorce lawyer practicing for more than thirty-five years, Susan Reach Winters has seen it all: couples who have broken up over crazy spending, controlling parents, cheating scandals—even dental work!

Susan established the Family Law Department at Budd Larner PC, a prestigious full-service law firm with offices in New Jersey and New York. From her experience working with hundreds of couples, Susan developed an innovative team approach to address the legal, financial, and emotional ramifications of divorce—combining the expertise of therapists, financial advisors, and attorneys to help her clients through their prenup and divorce negotiations and help them create fulfilling lives after their marriages end.

With broad experience in family law—including prenuptial agreements, divorce, child custody, spousal support, and equitable distribution—Susan has lectured extensively and written two legal books on the subject. She has been named among the Top 25 New Jersey Leading Women Entrepreneurs and New Jersey's Best 50 Women in Business and serves on the boards of several charitable foundations, including Dress for Success and the Runway of Dreams Foundation. She holds a BS from Rutgers University and a JD from Seton Hall University School of Law.

Susan can be reached at srw@thatwillneverhappentous.com.

CPSIA information can be obtained
at www.ICGtesting.com
Printed in the USA
FFHW012040090419
51638647-57065FF